D1030778

Advance Praise for *Pandemonium*

"This urgent wake-up call delivers a comprehensive, eye-opening analysis about China's master plan, in its quest for world domination, systematically to destroy our country. With the Chinese Communist Party's increasing military aggression and with its economic warfare aimed at the U.S., this timely and important book should shake up every American. In *Pandemonium: China's Global Strategy To Cripple America*, Curtis Ellis offers a brilliant plan to win—utilizing a "New Declaration Of Independence"—before it's too late. A must-read."

—**Naomi Wolf**, former Political Adviser to Al Gore and
Bill Clinton, CEO of DailyClout, and bestselling author
of *The Beauty Myth, The End of America*, and more.

"This compelling book by Curtis Ellis shows why he was a 'secret weapon' for our side against Chinese unfair trade practices. In *Pandemonium: China's Global Strategy to Cripple America*, Ellis lays out an ingenious plan to set America on a new path. A must read."

—**Michael Pillsbury**, Director of the Center on Chinese
Strategy at the Hudson Institute, US Defense Policy
Adviser, and bestselling author of *The Hundred-Year
Marathon: China's Strategy to Replace America*.

"There is no American future without a full-throated Declaration of Independence from the Chinese Communist Party, as the inspirational Curtis Ellis reminds us in this must-read critique of the 'elite merger' that has been taking place between the American and Chinese ruling classes. If anyone can be credited in their legacy for waking the populist West up to the extreme danger of the CCP, it is the late, great Curtis Ellis."

—**Raheem Kassam**, Editor-in-Chief of *The National Pulse*

"Two words always and easily come to mind when friends and colleagues think of Curtis Ellis—'admiration' and 'affection.' Admiration for his extraordinary and courageous work in alerting the democratic world to the China threat when few others noticed or cared. And "affection" because whether in government or outside we knew Curtis as not only a brainy man but one of charm and enormous good will towards others. We miss him greatly."

—**Anthony R Dolan**, Pulitzer Prize–winning reporter, former Chief Speechwriter to Ronald Reagan, former Senior Adviser to the Secretary of State, and former Special Assistant to President Donald Trump

"This insightful book—a great epitaph to a great life—exposes the folly of our nation's dangerous partnership with a totalitarian regime. Every American should read this."

—**Dr. Rob Spalding**, Brig Gen, USAF (R), former China Strategist for the Chairman of the Joint Chiefs of Staff at the Pentagon, and author of *Stealth War* and *War Without Rules*

"Curtis Ellis was a 'Passionate Crusader' against the UNFAIR TRADE AGREEMENTS and the 'Hollowing Out' of American Manufacturing. Early on Ellis recognized that China was an 'Existential Threat' to the USA and the world and worked to get this urgent message out to America. Curtis Ellis's voice of awareness and enlightenment shines through in this excellent book about China's strategy to DOMINATE the USA, both economically and militarily. He shows how to reset and halt that. His Patriotic legacy carries on, as strong as ever, and will not be forgotten…"

—**Dan DiMicco**, former Chairman of
Nucor Steel Corporation

"A trenchant call to arms about America's economic decline, China's part in it, and what we can do about it. Every concerned citizen should read this book."

—**Ian Fletcher**, economist and author of
Free Trade Doesn't Work

"Curtis Ellis was a patriot and longtime defender of American manufacturers and workers against unfair trade deals and neoliberal policies that offshored millions of jobs and hollowed out critical U.S. industries. This timely, important book is a gripping fact filled account of the looming threat the Chinese Communist Party poses to U.S. economic and national security. Ellis gives the way to counter this that includes a stirring 'New Declaration of Independence.' Curtis Ellis was an invaluable ally in this fight, and the legacy and work that he left behind will continue stronger than ever. Highly recommended."

—**Michael Stumo**, CEO of the Coalition
for a Prosperous America

"Having been involved in doing business with, and in China I can state that they 'Stack the Deck' against you. They demand that you supply them with the latest equipment and technology as well as your most advanced product and process designs. You can expect your return on investment to be break even at best. Curtis Ellis lays bare the frightening truth about the CCG in this carefully researched work that should shake American leaders up on how to deal with this threat. This incisive book should be in the hands of every businessperson, economist, policy maker—every American."

—**Michael Husar**, Director of Manufacturing Systems, Delphi Automotive Saginaw Steering Division

"When America needed Curtis Ellis, he was always there, speaking truth to power and exposing the corporate and political interests that were eager to abandon American principles, throw American workers under the bus, and transfer American capital and intellectual property to an aggressive authoritarian nation in exchange for short term profits. This clarion call details all that mischief but more importantly it offers us a path forward, where our nation can redeem and rebuild itself, free of the corrosive influence of the Chinese state."

—**Greg Autry, PhD.**, co-author of *Death by China*

"Curtis Ellis was one of the early policy experts to realize the danger the Communist Chinese Party posed to America. He understood the world economy and pointed out that 'free trade' was a fallacy because of the mercantilist, totalitarian dictatorship in China. Ellis worked with Peter Navarro to put together President Trump's 'Make America Great Again' program. *Pandemonium: China's Global Strategy to Cripple America* sounds the alarm on the gathering storm with a chilling account of China's assault on America in its quest for Superpower status. A crisis is inevitable with China's increasing aggression and frightening military buildup paid for by America's middle class. Ellis gives us a detailed, comprehensive and winning plan to overturn our relationship with the CCP in this eye-opening book every American should read."

—**Michele Nash-Hoff**, Vice President, Industry Reimagined 2030, and author of *Rebuild Manufacturing: The Key to American Prosperity*

"The U.S.-China relationship will continue to grow in importance for the next several decades. In that context, *Pandemonium: China's Global Strategy to Cripple America* should be on the nightstand of everyone interested in the subject. Policymakers who ignore Curtis Ellis's analysis—and his prescriptions—will do so at their peril."

—**Bill Pascoe**, longtime conservative activist

PANDEMONIUM

CHINA'S GLOBAL STRATEGY TO CRIPPLE AMERICA

CURTIS ELLIS

PREFACE BY STEVE BANNON
FOREWORD BY MAXINE ALBERT

POST HILL
PRESS

A POST HILL PRESS BOOK
ISBN: 979-8-88845-152-6
ISBN (eBook): 978-1-63758-912-0

Pandemonium:
China's Global Strategy to Cripple America
© 2023 by Maxine Albert
All Rights Reserved

Cover illustration by Yoni Limor, www.YoniLimor.com
Cover design by Cody Corcoran

Post Hill Press
New York • Nashville
posthillpress.com

Published in the United States of America
1 2 3 4 5 6 7 8 9 10

To Jack Davis and Maxine

CONTENTS

PREFACE BY STEVE BANNON

Curtis Ellis was an American Original...a man of ideas and a man of action; a thinker and a street fighter; a man as comfortable in a room of ironworkers as he was in a room of economists.

When the history of this time is written, Curtis Ellis will be remembered as an economic nationalist who answered the call and manned the ramparts early for the Make America Great Again, America First Movement. He was the first significant thinker and doer to come aboard a Trump team that was in dire need of both. Curtis Ellis knew the issues, Curtis Ellis knew the players, Curtis Ellis knew the traps.

Without that expertise the MAGA Movement could have well floundered. But instead, it flourished—driven by the Common Man listening to the ideas, nodding and saying, "I agree with that; that's what I've been thinking all along."

That link between common decency, common sense, and common cause is exactly where Curtis Ellis worked.

MAGA cannot thank him enough, I can't thank him enough, and generations to come—when they hold American jobs making American products in American factories—will not be able to thank him enough.

FOREWORD AND DEDICATION
BY MAXINE ALBERT

I met Curtis at a going-away party that I almost skipped. The room was crowded with men who blended together, a sea of gray, brown, and black suits. One man, however, stood out. He was in a striped sky-blue blazer, and the closer he came, I realized it even matched his eyes. *That* was attention to detail. *This* was a man who marched to the beat of his own drum.

It is extraordinary and humbling to think of how our lives are forever altered by moments we almost missed. If I hadn't gone to the party, I would not have met the brilliant mind and lively wit who became my best friend, partner, and the love of my life for nearly twenty-three years, right up until his death on February 14, 2021. It was just like Curtis to make sure I would always be thinking of "him" on Valentine's Day.

Curtis faced challenges in his valiant battle with cancer, but he was also not going to give up on a lifelong mission. He had started writing this book before his illness, and he was determined to finish it. He saw the Chinese Communist Party's looming aggression and hostile acts as the most dangerous threat to the nation he loved. And no one loved the United States more than Curtis. I realize many people *say* that, but Curtis *lived* it.

In his decades-long activism, he came to understand that China was the single biggest enemy of American workers. Curtis became the voice of the working man, relentless in his pursuit to bring manufacturing and jobs back to America. For him, it was about the preservation of dignity and a way of life as much as it was about a paycheck.

Curtis spent enough time in the proverbial trenches to realize that decent folks with no work and no hope because their jobs had been shipped overseas are an American tragedy. Once, a factory worker he was interviewing said to him, "You can tell me that this pair of boots costs less when it's made in China, but that doesn't matter to me. If I don't have a job, I don't care how much it costs, I can't afford it." As Curtis wryly noted, "He didn't need an economic degree to figure that one out." American workers deserved better. He would make it better.

Curtis was no detached analyst. He was a dedicated activist who lived his life according to his ideals. He put his money where his mouth was—he always bought "Made in America," and I once saw him pay twice as much for an air conditioner because it had that all-important qualification. Mom-and-pop shops were his go-to. He only bought chicken from a local farmer. I could list many more examples, but you get the idea.

Curtis had unwavering faith that if he told the *truth*, people would get it, even if his ideas were not in fashion. He was on to China's threat for years and years. And he got pushback when he called out the Chinese Communist Party, warning about its lies and the sellout of Wall Street and corporate America. It took courage and an outsized sense of right and wrong to go against the establishment. Curtis was up to the task. Through his impassioned writing, astute political commentary, and inspiring rhetoric at rallies, town halls, on TV and radio, he delivered a

well-researched, incisive truth about China's unfair trade practices as one of the key components to a long-term strategy to
weaken and overtake the U.S.

Every honest, true idea has its moment eventually. This one
came in 2016, as "trade abuse" and "China" came to the forefront
of the presidential campaign, thanks to Donald J. Trump. And
Curtis was a persuasive architect of this great awakening. In one
TV appearance, a pundit who had previously had a fiery clash
with him admitted, on air, that it was Curtis's thoughtful analysis
that had transformed his whole view of China's trade practices.

At one memorable panel at the Hudson Institute in
Washington, D.C., Michael Pillsbury, the think tank's director
for Chinese strategy, said that Curtis, a trade adviser to President
Trump, was a "secret weapon." Other panelists, from Beijing, had
spoken in favor of increased Chinese investment in American
communities. Curtis approached the podium in his inimitable
style: a confident smile and a glint in his eyes (he always loved
a good fight). After a droll chuckle, he began, "I find an offer by
China to invest in midwestern states affected by deindustrialization quite amusing," he said, "considering what the major cause
of deindustrialization in these states was." A mischievous laugh
punctuated the absurdity of the offer, and then Curtis proceeded
to knock down every assertion made by the preceding Chinese
panelists with the precision of a five-star general armed with
a battalion of indisputable facts. The moment was pure Curtis
Ellis—and so is this book.

With sharp and comprehensive analysis, Curtis lays out the
dark side of China's rise, its vision as an emerging superpower,
and its mission to cripple America. It is a chilling account, and
the stakes couldn't be higher. Curtis pushed himself to finish this
book because he saw something truly sinister in China's growing

aggression. He saw that this threat wasn't only about "trade abuse as economic warfare." This was—and is—about China's dramatic nuclear expansion, its escalating military buildup paid for by America's middle class. Crisis, he predicted, is inevitable.

But Curtis, ever hopeful, had a vision for a brighter future. In this book, you will find reminders of how our nation's successes were built on the principle of self-reliance, creating the greatest industrial power in the world; how far we have strayed from that path; and how we can get it back. Curtis lays out an ingenious plan for a paradigm shift with a new "Declaration of Independence" that will end America's dependence on China and set our nation on a new course.

Tens of thousands of workers today have jobs in manufacturing plants throughout the U.S. in large part due to policies put in place because of Curtis's activism and innovative thinking. But what I'll remember is the afternoon in the hospital when Curtis and I were talking and our conversation was interrupted by the patient in the next bed—"Are you Curtis Ellis?" I opened the curtain, and the man beamed. "I recognized your voice! I've seen you on TV, heard you on radio, and read your great articles. You are my hero!" The man was being treated for a September 11-related illness, and he was calling Curtis an inspiration.

Curtis was a true patriot who wanted to make our country a better place. He never gave up; he fought to the end. I'm so proud of him.

His courage, commitment, passion, and fierce determination were the very things that captured my heart. He taught me, as he taught many, how to be a better American. As I write these words, I can hear Curtis saying something he often told me: "Each of us has a part to play to stand up for America. You *can* change the world, one person at a time."

PROLOGUE

The coronavirus pandemic has shaken old institutions and challenged old ways. The international order as we have known it for thirty years is breaking.

An imperialist Chinese Communist Party seeks to bend the global economy to its own will and remake the world in its own image.

We face a moment of truth. Are we in this nation willing to watch our own way of life, our own liberties and livelihoods, grow dependent on policies made in Beijing?

For decades now, China has bent and abused and broken the rules of the international economic system to its own benefit. They have stolen our intellectual property and forced our companies to transfer sensitive trade secrets and technology. They have manipulated their currency and cheated time and again on their trade commitments. They have been complicit in the trafficking of persons and relied upon the forced labor of religious minorities.

And America has suffered. Since Beijing won Most Favored Nation status and joined the World Trade Organization in 2001, we have lost over three million jobs to China.

As a result, blue-collar workers go without work for months or years on end as their jobs are sent overseas. Wages flatline and fall. Families struggle for food, and middle-class neighborhoods collapse.

We were promised things would be different. We were told that giving China access to our markets would reform their behavior, make them more liberal. We were told it would be good for America and for the world. But the Chinese government systematically built its military on the backs of our middle class.

We cannot afford inaction any longer. If the coronavirus pandemic doesn't make that clear, nothing will. The United States must now reform the global economy to rebuild our strength. This nation must again take control of our own destiny.

The pandemic exposed a Grand Canyon-size fault in our economy. We don't make critical products in America anymore. It's a threat to our health, our national security, and our way of life. Americans have long known about this problem. Washington is just waking up to it, and Wall Street was hoping it wouldn't get caught. It's time to fix it. We need to invest in America again and protect our people.

The goal is simple—if we need it, we should make it.

The time has come for bold action to encourage domestic production, halt the damage to American workers and bring critical manufacturing supply chains back to this country from China and elsewhere. A wide range of industries have learned their operations are hostage to events far beyond their control so long as they rely on foreign countries for the production of critical inputs.

Never again should the American people find themselves vulnerable to the Chinese Communist Party for critical supplies and industrial components. Congress can immediately enact new local-content-requirement rules, requiring that manufacturers of finished products procure higher percentages of their inputs over time from domestic suppliers, for all industries selling to the federal government or essential to crisis response, chief among them medicine and medical equipment. Such requirements should be coupled with investment subsidies to assist firms struggling to source domestically from third parties but willing to build out input production themselves.

Federal policy should reward firms that invest in new domestic production facilities with federally backed, low-interest capital expenditure financing. A new departure is upon us. The old order is giving way. This moment is full of promise, if we have the courage to lead. To begin a new era, we must end the old.

The United States must seek new arrangements and new rules, in concert with other free nations, to restore America's economic sovereignty and again practice the capitalism that made us strong.

We can build a future of prosperity shared by all Americans, from our rural towns to the urban cores. We can build a future that ensures our national security in this new century.

We can build a future that gives confidence to American workers and the communities they call home.

With an economy that better suits our interests, that better protects our people, we can find the strength and purpose to counter the gravest danger to the American nation in a century, and to unleash again the promise of our unique and marvelous way of life.

Let the work begin in earnest to forge a new way forward.

INTRODUCTION

Americans lived in a global economy when we wrote the first Declaration of Independence.

At that time "the global economy" was known as the British Empire.

The British Empire touched the four corners of the Earth, and the sun never set on it. There were no borders in the British Empire. British ships ruled the waves. British industry ruled commerce. The King enforced a uniform set of rules controlling the flow of people, goods, and money throughout the realm.

In this borderless global economy ruled from London, people whose names are now legend—George Washington, Thomas Jefferson, Alexander Hamilton, Benjamin Franklin, Tom Paine, among others—decided America should be its own independent country.

The American Revolution was a rebellion against globalism.

Better we should govern ourselves and make our own rules that serve our own interests, not the interests of others somewhere else. Let them make their own rules. We'll make ours.

The rest, as they say, is history.

And so, twelve score and seven years ago the people of thirteen British colonies on the east coast of North America declared their independence from the British Empire.

The American Revolution was a trade war.

The colonists were prohibited from enjoying the fruits of their labors, what they grew, dug, and made with their own hands. They could not use the bounty of their plentiful farms, forests, and mines to make the clothing, furnishings, and ploughs their people needed.

Americans were compelled to send their fiber, timber, and ore on ships across the ocean to "the workshop of the world," where they were fashioned into finished goods, then sent back and sold to Americans at prices set by others. The people struggling to carve out a life for themselves in the New World were forced to buy essential goods from foreign shores.

Today, the "workshop of the world" is not Britain, but China. And just as the king of England wrote the rules that crippled American industries, the Communist Party of China is waging economic warfare against the United States.

China's industries, many of them owned outright by the government, dump their products in our country at prices far below the cost of production in order to drive American industry into extinction.

Swarms of Beijing's spies and cyberespionage actors steal our technology and trade secrets—the property of our citizens and the fruit of our intellectual and physical labor.

Beijing's rulers invited American companies to do business in China, then forced them to hand over their property and earnings. They waged war against our values and our God-given rights, threatening reprisals on Americans who speak freely about the true nature of the Chinese Communist Party (CCP).

They threatened and withheld the lifesaving medical supplies American companies have either made in China or purchased from China.

They waged chemical warfare against our people, producing and exporting deadly drugs that kill tens of thousands of Americans year after year, ravaging our families and laying waste to entire communities.

They waged biological warfare on America. Deliberately, through incompetence and corruption, the CCP unleashed a deadly virus on the world that took a toll in lives and treasure and brought our country to a standstill.

The coronavirus pandemic made clear something that started a long time ago: we have grown dangerously dependent on China for our health, our well-being, and our very way of life.

Two hundred forty-seven years ago, Americans recognized the cost of being dependent on a foreign power. Fifty years ago, we learned the cost of being dependent on foreign energy when the oil sheiks cut us off. Lines stretched for miles at gas stations, and often there was no gasoline to be had at any price.

Now, we've learned the cost of being dependent on foreign manufacturing. Americans could not get the medical supplies we needed to protect ourselves. We were at the mercy of China, the place where our factories had moved.

And the problem is not limited to just medical supplies. So many other products we use every day, from smartphones to automobile parts, disappeared from America as factories in China shut down.

Our dependence on communist China didn't happen overnight. It took many years, decades actually, and was the result of decisions, deception, complacency, and delusion.

The CCP took advantage of our good intentions. Some of our leaders had a naïve belief that doing business with the People's Republic of China, raising the standard of living of the Chinese people with Western investment, would magically transform a communist dictatorship into a peace-loving democracy. Our leaders wanted to believe what happened in Japan and Germany after World War II would happen in China after the Cold War.

And the Chinese Communist Party wanted us to believe that too.

The communists lied to our political and business leaders, promising a rich market for American products—if we gave China the factories and know-how to make those products. Those factories ended up making goods to sell to the American people, rather than American factories selling to the Chinese.

Our political leaders had also come to believe that the world would be better without nations or borders, that we would all be better off. They allowed, even encouraged, our factories to move to China.

And the Chinese Communist Party wanted us to believe that too.

They said they believed in "free trade" and "globalization" even as they built tariff walls to keep American-made products out and sought global supremacy for the Chinese nation under communist rule.

Our business leaders had a misguided focus on immediate profits. That led them to outsource our jobs and industries and blinded them to the devastating consequences for our people and our nation. But the American people understood what those at the top refused to see.

Now everyone sees the true cost of the China price.

Now no one can deny communist China has ill intentions toward us.

The CCP is a Marxist-Leninist party that believes in a communist "dictatorship of the proletariat." It has absolute control over all institutions in China, including the government, military, courts, media, culture and business. The individual, society and the economy exist to support the party. Freedom of speech, of the press, of religion, of assembly and the right to own property do not exist.

The CCP believes its monopoly control of economic, political and social activity is superior to all other forms of government and seeks to impose its system on the world.

Americans understand it is necessary to loosen the bonds that have tied us to the Communist regime in China.

Americans understand we must do as we did over two centuries ago: cut our ties to a foreign tyranny and establish our independence.

When in the Course of human events, it becomes necessary for one people to dissolve the political bands which have connected them with another, and to assume among the powers of the earth, the separate and equal station to which the Laws of Nature and of Nature's God entitle them, a decent respect to the opinions of mankind requires that they should declare the causes which impel them to the separation....

...When a long train of abuses and usurpations, pursuing invariably the same Object evinces a design to reduce them under absolute Despotism, it is their right, it is their duty, to throw off such Government, and to provide new Guards for their future security.

—Declaration of Independence, 1776

In fourteen hundred ninety-two, Columbus sailed the ocean blue. The global economy is nothing new.

—Anonymous

CHAPTER I

How America Became An Invalid

How did we become dependent on others for food, clothing, medicine, and just about everything else life depends on? How did a self-reliant nation, the land of the free and the home of the brave, become an invalid?

We didn't get here overnight. It took time.

It wasn't always like this.

We used to make the things we bought and bought the things we made.

We used to wear clothing sewn in Los Angeles and the Garment District of New York from fabric woven in the Carolinas from cotton grown in Mississippi. Not so much anymore.

We used to make socks in Alabama and towels in North Carolina. Not anymore.

We used to make shoes in New Hampshire. Not anymore.

We used to make cars in Michigan and the parts that went into them in Milwaukee, Wisconsin; Moraine, Ohio; and Lockport, New York. Not anymore.

Why is that?

Politicians and "experts" with postgraduate degrees from the finest schools tell us it was inevitable, the result of forces beyond our control: "globalization," "technology," "the internet," "the world coming closer together after the end of the Cold War."

They say it had to be this way. Accept it. Get used to it.

They are wrong.

Our present state of helplessness didn't "just happen." It was not inevitable. It was the result of specific decisions made by specific people in specific places and specific positions of power.

These people *sent* our jobs and entire industries overseas. They made the decision to put American workers and farmers in direct competition with workers and farmers in other countries who earn far less than Americans. In that competition, we lost.

You didn't lose your job—it was taken from you. America didn't lose her industries–they were taken from her.

More than seventy thousand U.S. factories have closed since Congress approved the North American Free Trade Agreement (NAFTA) that went into effect in 1994 and opened trade with communist China in 2001.

Corporate executives decided to move factories to China or another low-cost country so they could skip paying American wages and taxes and avoid our environmental, health, and safety rules.

Some of the money they saved went into their own pockets as executive bonuses.

Some went, as campaign contributions, into the pockets of the Washington politicians who passed the laws giving the green light to move to communist China.

And some went to the "experts" at colleges, universities, and think tanks that preach the religion of globalism and globalization.

Washington and the politicians who thrive there became converts. Under the spell of globalization, they sent our jobs and industries to various countries and, finally, to communist China.

The origins of globalism and its hold on Washington go back nearly eighty years, to the aftermath of World War II.

America had the strongest, maybe the only, industrial economy left standing. Western Europe was in ruins, Japan was digging out of radioactive ashes, and Eastern Europe was under the boot of Joseph Stalin.

We were in a Cold War that pitted the U.S. against the communist giants of Soviet Russia and Red China. In this battle against communism, the State Department saw trade deals as a way to advance their geostrategic foreign policy.

We would allow Japan, Europe, and other allies to sell their goods in the U.S. even as they shut American goods out of their markets. We'd give up American jobs to build middle-class societies in countries that would become our allies. The State Department would buy friends around the world.

The strategy was a success at building middle-class societies from Greece to Japan. The only problem was it destroyed large chunks of our middle class in the process.

One of the other battlegrounds was the Third World. Would these newly independent nations, the former colonies of Britain and France in Africa and Asia, join the communist bloc or "the free world"?

In 1960, Governor Ernest "Fritz" Hollings of South Carolina was on to the game.

Hollings warned the Democratic candidate for president, John F. Kennedy, that textile imports were devastating his state.

Even after the countries destroyed by World War II had rebuilt, "the State Department continues to try winning friends by encouraging the export of American technology and productive capacity," said Hollings, "and that means loss of jobs here at home." Giving a trade advantage became part of foreign aid.

"Our State Department plus the international banks and multinational giants push for international welfare under the umbrella of 'free trade.'"

"Over at the Department of State," Hollings pointed out, "there is an Asian Desk, a European Desk, an African Desk, etc—but there is no American Desk to represent strongly the interests of the United States," Hollings wrote. "This has caused tremendous damage to some of our basic industries."

The textile industry was the largest employer of women and minorities in America, and the imports were hurting those groups the most.

Hollings's words fell on deaf ears.

While President Kennedy pledged he would protect the textile industry, he instead pushed the Trade Expansion Act of 1962. Not content giving trade concessions to our Cold War allies in Europe and Japan, Kennedy declared it a moral duty to "open our markets to the developing countries of the Third World in Africa, Asia, and Latin America."

Decade after decade, under Democratic and Republican presidents, Washington continued sacrificing industry after industry, from textiles and furniture to consumer electronics, metals, and advanced technology.

1967: The Summer of Free Love and Free Trade

San Francisco, June 1967, the Summer of Love. Flower children flocked to the city's Haight-Ashbury district envisioning a world united in peace, love, and understanding.

A continent away in Washington, D.C., the Joint Economic Committee of the U.S. Congress held a hearing on "The Future of U.S. Foreign Trade Policy."

The witnesses were some of the most powerful men in America. They laid out their vision for society, a plan as radical as anything that had ever been proposed in the history of the American republic. In some ways, it was surprisingly similar to the acid dreams of those in the Haight-Ashbury.

A *Congressional Record* transcript of the proceedings reveals the road map Washington followed for the subsequent fifty years, a journey that left our jobs and industries by the side of the road and made us dependent on other countries for even the most basic essentials of life.

We see from the testimony that so-called "free trade" agreements such as NAFTA were never really about trade between nations.

No, the real goal of U.S. "trade" policy was to weaken—if not eliminate—sovereign, independent nations and concentrate power in the hands of global corporations and their factotums in international organizations.

No member of Congress present at the hearing, neither Republican nor Democrat, challenged this plan that undermined the independence of the United States of America.

Their silence was consent, and their consent became the consensus, the accepted bipartisan wisdom that reigned unchallenged in Washington.

At the hearing, George Ball, a Wall Street grandee who served in the State Department under presidents Kennedy and Johnson, laid out the ideology of globalism:

"Earth-straddling corporations" should replace the "crazy quilt" of independent nations as the organizing principle for society. The will citizens express through elected representatives is an obstacle. Economic and social policy should be made by international organizations, "supranational" authorities, not national governments that answer to citizens.

Ball praised stateless corporations as "one of our major accomplishments since the war." He explained they operate as if there were no nations or borders, as if the "world economy were a fact." He told the lawmakers they should "shape our governmental action so as to help give reality to that assumption."

For the benefit of the senators and congressmen who perhaps didn't understand, Ball explained the magic of what we now call "global supply chains":

> Today a corporate management in Detroit or New York or London or Dusseldorf may decide that it can best serve the market of country Z by combining the resources of country X with labor and plan facilities in country Y—and it may alter that decision six months from now.

But a cloud darkened Ball's vision of a perfect world: nations and borders!

> To fulfill its full potential, the multinational corporation must be able to operate with little regard for national boundaries—or, in other words, for restrictions imposed by individual national governments.

Luckily, Ball had the solution. Washington should work for "*a considerable erosion of the rigid concepts of national sovereignty,*" to eliminate the "antiquated political structures in which most of the world is organized."

In plain English, he wanted to get rid of independent, sovereign nations, or, as he dismissively described them, *"the present crazy quilt of small national states."*

Understand, it's not personal. It's strictly business:

> Business decisions are frustrated by a multiplicity of different restrictions by relatively small nation states that are based on parochial considerations, reflect no common philosophy, and are keyed to no common goal.

Ball dismissed national interests as frustrating "parochial considerations." The "common philosophy" and "common goal" should be economic efficiency and corporate profits, not the principle that people everywhere have a right to govern themselves and determine their own destinies.

In the economically integrated world George Ball envisioned, the important decisions—what you do for a living, how much you earn—are made by global corporatist technocrats, without interference from elected governments that answer to citizens.

That is the ideology of globalism explained in its entirety.

Most of what he described fifty years ago has come to pass.

The End of the Cold War: Globalism Über Alles

When the Cold War ended with the fall of the Berlin Wall, Washington found a new rationale for the same old policies. Before the fall, they said free trade would stop communism.

After the fall, they said free trade would ensure world peace for all eternity.

But the new rationale wasn't really new. It came straight from the nineteenth-century British Empire, where Richard Cobden, a textile manufacturer and member of Parliament, preached the gospel of free trade with religious fervor.

Cobden believed free trade would not just lead to more commerce—it would end war forever. He envisioned "the greatest revolution that ever happened in the world's history." Armies, empires, even national boundaries would become extinct.

In 1846, Cobden delivered his famous "I have a dream speech" describing how free trade:

> shall act on the moral world as the principle of gravitation in the universe, drawing men together, thrusting aside the antagonism of race, and creed, and language, and uniting us in the bonds of eternal peace.
>
> I believe that the desire and the motive for large and mighty empires; for gigantic armies and great navies—for those materials which are used for the destruction of life and the desolation of the rewards of labour—will die away; I believe that such things will cease to be necessary, or to be used, when man becomes one family.

The twentieth century and two world wars proved Cobden wrong. France and Germany were major trading partners before they became major sparring partners. In our own time, Russia and Ukraine were number-one besties on the trade front until, well, you know what happened there.

But, like zombies, bad ideas never die, and Cobden's belief that countries that trade with each other would not go to war with each other remains popular with the smart set even to this day, despite all evidence to the contrary. Policymakers on the *Acela* corridor between Washington and Wall Street take it as an item of faith.

The big idea was appealingly simple, even though it wasn't true: globalization, aka "free trade," will make all countries rich, and once rich, they will be more democratic and peace loving.

(We put "free trade" in quotes because it isn't "free." It's managed trade, and it isn't even really "trade" either. It's about moving investments and factories, not goods, between countries.)

Washington Pays to Move Companies Offshore

The State Department's old "trade for aid" idea had such appeal, our government didn't just give jobs away—it actually paid others to take them.

Just ask Elicia Jo Stain, who used to live and work in Decaturville, Tennessee, a one-stop-sign town halfway between Nashville and Memphis, home to 849 souls today.

"The Government used our tax dollars to take our jobs away from us," she says.

Decaturville Sportswear employed fifteen hundred people making women's sportswear for J. C. Penney and Sears in the 1970s. The company was always profitable.

The plant closed in 1991 after the U.S. Agency for International Development (USAID) helped Decaturville Sportswear move to El Salvador.

USAID paid to build a $5 million plant in El Salvador and on top of that gave the company low-interest loans and $1.1 million in insurance to help grease the skids.

The new factory in El Salvador did the exact same work as the plant in Decaturville. The only difference? Workers in El Salvador earned about a tenth that of the Decaturville workers.

USAID justified its treachery against American workers with the contention that economic development would promote stable democratic governments in Central America. Right.

Decaturville wasn't alone. Federal subsidies helped fifty-seven other clothing factories close and move to Central America, taking twelve thousand jobs with them in the early '90s, the *New York Times* reported at the time.

USAID shut down its program, nicknamed "Trade Not Aid," after the political heat became too much, but Washington has a grab bag of programs that trade away American jobs.

Congress approved the General System of Preferences,[1] (GSP) in 1974. It's America's oldest and largest trade-for-aid program and continues to this day.

This scheme, hatched in the United Nations,[2] lets the poorest countries in the world sell their goods in the U.S. duty-free.

Thanks to GSP, the U.S. became the biggest market for many of India's industries.

When Congress enacted the program forty-nine years ago, India was desperately poor. Its people had few opportunities to earn a living above subsistence level.

But that was before the personal computer, the internet, call centers, and software coding. Now, India uses brainpower and technology to replace American IT and service-sector workers the same way communist China uses subsidies and forced labor to replace American manufacturing workers.

Today, half of India's 1.4 billion people are in the middle class.

Yet for years Washington bureaucrats refused to acknowledge the world was changing and continued to treat India like the basket case of a half-century ago.

And Here We Are...

Washington's policymakers dreamed of what was good for "the global economy" rather than what was good for America. Other nations took advantage of our naïveté and good intentions and did what was good for their citizens.

At the same time, global corporations jumped at the chance to replace well-paid American labor with cheap foreign labor.

Our leaders in politics, business, and academia sacrificed American jobs on the altar of globalism and told us, perhaps even believing it themselves, this would make us all rich.

And they applied this wishful thinking to communist China.

They told us doing business with the communist dictatorship would end its human rights abuses, close its prison camps, and stop its religious persecution, forced abortions, and military buildup.

But as our capital and technology transformed China into an economic superpower, it did not become more democratic or peace-loving.

China imprisons millions of Muslims in concentration camps. It still exploits prison labor, forces women to abort babies, demolishes churches, persecutes Christians, and oppresses all people of faith.

It's become clear that giving China our industries endangered our health and well-being—and the world's.

Corporate globalism has failed Americans, failed the Chinese people, and failed the world.

It is time to reassert our independence, prioritize the needs of our people, and do what's best for America.

That's how we will repair the damage our country has suffered and repair the world.

For when we are stronger, we are better able to help others and ensure our ideals of freedom, liberty, and tolerance can be a light to the world for the ages.

CHAPTER II

A Dysfunctional Relationship

From toys to footwear, from auto parts to electronics, in one industry after another, China's state-controlled companies have captured market share in the U.S. and around the world.

Naïve observers and professional prevaricators like to paint the People's Republic of China's economic rise as a miracle of free market capitalism.

Nothing could be further from the truth.

A story in the *New York Times*[3] details how the Chinese Communist Party used subsidies, extortion, and a militarized labor force to become the world's iPhone factory.

When CCP officials decided to capture smartphone manufacturing on a global scale, they made Apple an offer it couldn't refuse.

China's communist government spent more than $1.5 billion to build an iPhone factory and barracks for the workers toiling there on land it grabbed from its previous residents. It paved roads, erected power plants, covered the transportation and energy costs for the factory, and paid bonuses for meeting export targets.

And there's more.

China eliminated corporate taxes on Apple for five years, then cut them in half for five more. It lent the company a quarter of a billion dollars, and then spent another $10 billion to build an airport near the iPhone plant for shipping parts and products in and out.

In a one-party state where independent unions and strikes are illegal, China's communist authorities guaranteed a regimented, militarized workforce, recruiting, training, and housing the factory's employees.

Anyone can see this is not free market capitalism at work. It is a state-directed economy, and the iPhone story shows what the CCP will do to capture a strategic industry, at any cost.

Drug pushers give away samples to get users hooked. China's tax and subsidy giveaways enticed Western companies, and they soon were hooked. They would do anything to keep their supplier happy. When Beijing demanded companies turn over blueprints and technology, they complied.

When Beijing was no longer content to be the world's low-end factory and sought to move up the manufacturing value chain, Western companies invested in China's state-backed enterprises, built research and development centers, and helped Beijing develop high-end manufacturing.

So much for the blithe assurances that America could let go of factory jobs in "sunset industries" because we would always hold on to R&D. Those who understand manufacturing knew better. They know research is tied to the shop, and when production went overseas, research and development would soon follow.

As China's economic power grew, so too did its cultural influence.

That's crucial because the CCP does not share our values. It does not tolerate freedom of religion, freedom of speech, individual liberty, private property, or any of the basic rights we consider fundamental.

Western companies that entrusted their economic future to the Chinese Communist Party soon subordinated American values to their profit interest. Told not to criticize Beijing's crackdown on pro-democracy protestors in Hong Kong, or its imprisonment of two million of its people in concentration camps, or its hacking and theft, they readily complied rather than risk retaliation by the CCP.

Economic ties with China became the rope the Communist Party used to strangle American workers, American businesses—and America itself.

The story of Washington's love affair with Beijing began in earnest in 1980.

President Jimmy Carter had opened formal diplomatic relations with Beijing a year earlier following President Richard Nixon's initial opening to China in 1972. Nixon thought he could play Beijing off against the Soviet Union, our primary adversary in the Cold War.

When the Soviet Red Army invaded Afghanistan in 1980, Beijing sided with the U.S., openly providing diplomatic support and secretly supplying weapons to the Afghan mujahedeen fighting the Soviet invaders.

Congress and the Carter administration moved to reward Beijing with Most Favored Nation trade status. That would give the communist regime the same low-tariff preferential trade treatment as our closest allies.

There was not much drama as Congress shambled toward giving its assent. Two themes emerged in the debate.

"The need for United States–Chinese cooperation in check-ing…the massive Soviet invasion of Afghanistan" was one ra-tionale. Another was the "potential market for U.S. goods in the People's Republic of China with its nearly one billion inhabitants."

Trade with China would be good for America strategically and economically, we were told.

Over on the House side, one of the few opponents, Repre-sentative John Rousselot of California, wasn't buying the sales pitch.

He saw China's communists as "really not much different from Russia" and suspected China was only interested in ob-taining America's high technology and would not "treat us any different than other dictatorial societies…once they've picked our brains." His was a distinctly minority view, but as it turned out, he was right.

However, Congress decided normal trade relations should begin as soon as possible, with the condition that China's Most Favored Nation status had to be renewed annually.

"Normal" trade relations continued unquestioned until Chairman Deng Xiaoping, who had been considered a reformer, unleashed his troops to massacre a still-unknown number of pro-democracy protestors at Tiananmen Square in 1989.

After that, Congress made several attempts to explicitly link China's Most Favored Nation status to its human rights record. President George H. W. Bush vetoed them all.

President Bush did sign watered-down legislation banning sales of equipment to the People's Liberation Army and placed controls on "dual use" technology with military applications, but he was careful not to upset trade relations with China.

In fact, Bush went so far as to send a groveling letter[4] to Deng apologizing for having done anything that could maybe possibly undermine U.S.–China relations. "I will leave what followed [the protests] to the history books…the actions that I took as President of the United States could not be avoided. As you know the clamor for stronger action remains intense. I resisted that clamor."

The Washington foreign policy experts had convinced themselves that despite the mass murder in Tiananmen Square, Deng was a "reformer," not a "hard-liner." Whatever we did, "It was important not to respond in a way that played into the hands of the hard-liners," Secretary of State James Baker said.

William Hawkins writes,[5] "keeping the door open to 'trade' with a regime that was not going to reform in its most fundamental ways was a strategic blunder of unprecedented scope. President Bush's reaction sent a message to American firms that it was not only permitted to transfer capital, jobs, and technology to China, but it was to be encouraged as the way to build a progressive Chinese society and tame the communist regime."

But our investments were not building a "progressive" China. We were not taming a dictatorial regime but strengthening it. And following Tiananmen Square, we were telling the CCP there would be no consequences for its atrocities. Appeasement only encourages further abuses.

"We should recall that the London Stock Exchange sent a congratulatory message to Neville Chamberlain after the 1938 Munich conference which marked the peak of appeasement towards Nazi Germany," Hawkins writes. President Bush and American business sent their congratulations to Chairman Deng.

In the 1992 campaign, candidate Bill Clinton slammed Bush for coddling the "butchers of Beijing." He promised he would be tougher and link the annual renewal of trade relations to improvements in the CCP's human rights record.

After Clinton was elected, Beijing enlisted allies in business and Wall Street to convince the new president to change course. This is an example of classical Chinese military strategy—use influential advisers in your opponent's leadership circle to turn your opponent's house on itself.

In *The Hundred-Year Marathon: China's Secret Strategy to Replace America as the Global Superpower*,[6] Michael Pillsbury details "the Clinton coup." Beijing played Robert Rubin, then chairman of the National Economic Council; Harvard economist Larry Summers, undersecretary of the Treasury; and other "free trade" acolytes in the president's camp to persuade Clinton to give China preferential access to our market and technology.

Beijing promised leading businessmen lucrative deals worth hundreds of millions of dollars. Major campaign donors lobbied the president, asking him not do anything that would interfere with selling Boeing aircraft or launching American satellites on Chinese rockets. Beijing used Clinton's own people as its unwitting accomplices to achieve its goal.

It worked. President Clinton abandoned his tough line. Like Bush and Carter and Ford before him, he expanded economic ties with China in the belief that doing so would turn the communist dictatorship into a free market social democracy.

The World Bank provided China's communist government with an economic strategy to catch up the United States while the U.S. government handed over sensitive technology, military know-how, intelligence, and expert advice. Wall Street prodded American companies to invest more and more in China.

A Senate investigation found[7] the Chinese government launched a covert operation in 1996 to use political donations to gain access to and influence politicians at the local, state, and federal level.

After the election, as the end of his last term approached, President Clinton moved to eliminate the annual review of China's human rights record. In 2000, backed by leading Republicans and Democrats, he asked Congress to grant China "permanent normal trade relations."

Permanent normal trade relations with Beijing would give corporate America the long-term certainty it needed to invest up to the hilt in China and replace well-paid American workers with Chinese workers earning eighteen cents an hour.

Business interests had essentially recruited Bill Clinton to push the China trade policy that benefited them.

The White House set up a China War Room with a staff of 150 government employees pulled from various federal departments. They coordinated with the Business Coalition for U.S.-China Trade, the U.S. Chamber of Commerce, and other business associations on an unprecedented lobbying effort.

The coalition took the themes from the earlier 1980 debate and fine-tuned them. *Trade with China was in America's national interest* because China had a billion new customers for American products. It would "enhance our national security" because "economic interdependence would lead states to trade, rather than war, with one another."

The U.S.-China Business Council also played a variation on "the 1980s wants its foreign policy back" theme, calling the annual human rights review a Cold War–era "relic of the confrontation with the Soviet Union." Today, the CCP plays the same melody, accusing American critics of having a "Cold War mentality."

President Clinton's commerce secretary, Bill Daley, recalls President Clinton spending "an incredible amount of time" speaking to business groups and buttonholing dozens of members of Congress. "I've never seen as much energy and focus on an issue," Daley said.

And Clinton wasn't alone in this unprecedented lobbying campaign.

Daley was visiting twenty House members a week and calling as many as twenty more every day. Vice President Al Gore, Secretary of State Madeline Albright, Defense Secretary William Cohen, Agriculture Secretary Dan Glickman, National Security Adviser Sandy Berger, and U.S. Trade Representative Charlene Barshefsky were among the top administration officials pushing the economic interest of the business coalition, selling trade with China as being in the national interest.

The seamless collaboration between the White House and the business lobbyists prompted an investigation into possible violations of the prohibition against using federal funds for "publicity or propaganda" and grassroots lobbying.

The bipartisan pro-China coalition included multinational business interests, Wall Street financiers, Democrats, and Republicans. It was a truly bipartisan effort.

Opposition also spanned the political spectrum. When the Senate debate opened, conservative Republican firebrand Jesse Helms of North Carolina and liberal Democratic icon Paul Wellstone of Minnesota stood on the same side. They knew China's communist regime posed a threat to American workers and American values.

They didn't want to do business with a regime that murdered peaceful pro-democracy demonstrators in Tiananmen square; that arrested independent union leaders; that used prisoner labor in its export industries; that imprisoned and persecuted Christians, Muslims, and Buddhists for practicing their religion;

and that performed forced abortions on women right up to the final days of pregnancy.

Senator Helms called permanent normal trade relations "the most ill-advised piece of legislation to come to the Senate floor in my twenty-eight years as a member of this body." Senators recognized they were about to take the most important vote of their careers.

Senators Helms, Wellstone, and others offered amendment after amendment to hold the CCP accountable for its religious persecution, prison labor, forced abortions, and labor rights violations.

Their amendments[8] show how little has changed in twenty years.

Then, the Chinese Communist Party was arbitrarily arresting, torturing, and executing thousands of Uighur Muslims in northwest China. Now, it has imprisoned millions rather than thousands in "reeducation" concentration camps. These prisoners are sent to factories to make goods for Apple, Nike, and other brands.

Then, as now, the Chinese Communist Party was harassing, incarcerating, and torturing "people on the basis of their religion," and closing and demolishing "mosques, temples, seminaries, Catholic churches, and Protestant "house churches."

Then, as now, the Chinese communist bosses imprisoned union leaders and organizers.

Then, as now, "violence against women exists in the People's Republic of China, including coercive family planning practices such as forced abortion and forced sterilization, prostitution, discrimination against women, trafficking in women and children, abuse of children, and discrimination against the disabled and minorities."

Senator Paul Wellstone, possibly the most progressive, pro-union senator ever, warned American manufacturing would be destroyed as multinational corporations moved U.S. factories to China.

Senator Joe Biden dismissed Wellstone, saying, "Nor do I see a collapse of the American manufacturing economy, as China, a nation with the impact on the world economy about the size of the Netherlands, suddenly becomes our major economic competitor."

All the warnings from Helms, Wellstone, and the others proved to be prophetic. Everything they said would go wrong has gone wrong.

Washington slept as China "picked our brain" and rose to become "our major economic competitor," as it built a military machine, grabbed neighbors' territory, and fortified its totalitarian dictatorship.

Washington slept, but what's afflicting Washington is not just narcolepsy—it is venality.

Senator Helms said expanding trade with China would serve the business interests of the corporate sector, but the Senate "must not confuse business interests with the national interest of the American people."

Our leaders ignored his warning. Many used their political connections to establish their own personal business interests in China. Henry Kissinger, Madeline Albright, and Diane Feinstein[9] (with her husband Richard Blum) are just a few of the influential policymakers who have made millions from investments in China.

Our political, academic, and financial leaders insisted China was a partner, not a competitor, because China was a partner in their own businesses. They confused their personal interests with the national interest of America.

Like the global corporations that sent jobs, capital, and technology to communist China, the politicians who helped them do it also got rich selling out the American people.

And many still don't understand the danger.

Upton Sinclair said, "It is difficult to get a man to understand something when his salary depends on his not understanding it."

History will record our collaboration with the CCP as the greatest error in American history.

U.S. trade relations with China have resulted in the greatest transfer of wealth in human history.

The Chinese government's industrial subsidies, espionage, and forced technology transfer have destroyed millions of jobs and entire cities across our country.

Chinese fentanyl has killed more Americans than the Iraq and Afghanistan wars combined.

Elected officials in both parties have let this happen.

Now, Beijing's rulers seek to make their totalitarian values, which are inimical to our own, the global norm.

More than fifty years ago, Ronald Reagan warned that freedom is never more than one generation away from extinction. We must fight for it, protect it, and defend it or else we may well spend our sunset years telling our children and our children's children what it once was like in America when men were free.

Today, those words are truer than ever.

CHAPTER III

Meet the New Boss: The Global Elite

At one time, the American businessman, the factory owner, and the corporate executive felt a bond to his community, his town, city, and nation.

The business operated not just to make a profit, though that was essential. It filled a need for its customers, which is why they willingly handed over their money, and it provided sustenance not just to its owners but to its employees and their families, to the suppliers and service providers that supported the company's existence, and to their employees and families. The taxes paid by the businesses and families supported schools, police, roads, courts, water and sewer systems, and so forth all the way up the ladder to our Army, Navy, Air Force, and Marines.

In short, a company was seen as an asset to its owners, its employees, the community, and the nation. What was good for business was good for America.

The patriotic businessman who feels a responsibility to his community, his state, and his nation is now an endangered species, if not extinct.

Corporate CEOs used to consider employees, suppliers, customers, community, and society as well as shareholders in their decisions. Now, their only consideration is how to make as much money as possible for shareholders or, as the management consultants put it, how to "maximize shareholder value."

And "shareholders" are not little old ladies in Florida waiting for their dividend checks in the mail.

No, they are Wall Street bankers, index funds, and money managers that control millions of shares. The "shareholder" is often the CEO himself, compensated with blocks of stock in the company he manages. That CEO "shareholder" profits personally when he pumps up the price of his stock by replacing Americans earning twenty dollars an hour with Chinese earning twenty dollars a week.

People—human beings who love their families, the places they live, and the culture they grew up with—don't enter into the corporate executive's decisions.

As corporate conglomerates grew larger and larger, their tentacles reaching all over the map, executives managing these enterprises came to feel no loyalty to our nation or any nation.

Thomas Paine wrote that commerce diminishes the spirit of patriotism. Thomas Jefferson put a finer point on it: "Merchants have no country. The mere spot they stand on does not constitute so strong an attachment as that from which they draw their gains."

"What's Good for the Global Economy" Replaced "What's Good for America"

The multinational corporation has become a stateless entity, a power unto itself, stronger than any government, with a single-minded mission of maximizing its profits.

And as these stateless, rootless corporations gained power in Washington, "The World" replaced "The United States" as the frame of reference for policymakers.

"What's good for the global economy" replaced "what's good for America" as the principle guiding our trade negotiators, policymakers, and diplomats. They set out to build a web of international trade agreements that facilitated the operations of globe-straddling corporations.

California Congressman Bertrand Gearhardt described Washington's trade negotiators in 1947 as "boatloads of smug diplomats, all-wise economists, experts, theorists, specialists, and whatnots eager to barter away the little factory in Wichita, the little shop in Keokuk."

These smug diplomats and all-wise economists sought an efficient, borderless world where people, goods, and money would flow freely. They were not interested in preserving small, privately owned local businesses or self-rule for the United States, with a government of the people, by the people, and for the people.

In the rarefied air at the pinnacles power, it was believed modern society had grown too complex for it to be governed by common people through representative democracy and sovereign nations; it would be better for trained specialists with a global perspective to manage the world "for the common good."

Of course, no one came right out and told the American people our form of government, the one we were taught about in school, was being replaced.

The experts and theorists pursued their plan without a congressional debate or vote. Quietly, stealthily, one stone at a time, they laid the groundwork for their Tower of Babel, expecting their edifice would be complete before anyone knew what had been built around them.

An "End Run Around National Sovereignty"

In "The Hard Road to World Order,"[10] Richard Gardner, a respected diplomat who served as President Clinton's ambassador to Spain, explained, "The 'house of world order' will have to be built from the bottom up.... An end run about national sovereignty, eroding it piece by piece, will accomplish much more than a frontal assault."

The European Union demonstrates how it's done. The EU began as a simple pact for trading coal and steel between France and Germany. Over the decades, it grew, brick by brick, into a twenty-seven-nation super state whose central bureaucracy regulates everything from food labeling to immigration policy—powers once held by Europe's national governments.

The "free flow of people, goods, and money" was the goal of the EU's founders. This was also the goal of the Trans-Pacific Partnership, designed to merge the economies of twelve nations on four continents, including the U.S. (President Trump withdrew the United States from the agreement in 2017.)

Prime Minister Shinzo Abe of Japan stood next to President Obama in 2015 and stated the Trans-Pacific Partnership would create "a new economic sphere in which *people, goods, and money will flow freely* in the Asia-Pacific region." [emphasis added]

"The free flow of people, goods, and money"—right from the Treaty of Rome,[11] the document that established the European Union.

Bye-Bye, American Citizenship

All this confirms the suspicions of Congressman Gearhardt, who predicted, "When the truth is told and the facts become known, the trade-agreements program will be revealed as...no less than a plot to merge the American economy with that of the world. This, despite an inevitable destruction of our standard of living, our high wage scales, and our most favorable working conditions, in all of which is inextricably involved the American way of life."

Strobe Talbott, Bill Clinton's Oxford roommate who went on to serve as his deputy secretary of state, described the future he and his colleagues envisioned, saying that in the coming years nationhood would be replaced by one global authority. Talbott wrote those words in 1992. Thirty-one years later, we have the Global Citizen organization with a community of millions that believe in one world without borders.

A post-national, even post-democratic mindset guides the experts who advise business and political leaders. Corporate consultants like McKinsey & Company have grown fat advising American businesses to cut costs by moving to China, even though doing so empowers a dictatorship and leaves American communities without jobs, revenues, and opportunities.

The globalist ideology has corrupted all of Washington. Stateless corporations and foreign governments run influence-peddling operations through a shell game of think tanks, lobbyists, banks, and Wall Street investment houses.

Nonprofit think tanks funded by globalist interests turn out op-eds and white papers pushing policies premised on "what's good for the global economy." Corporate lobbyists then cite this "expert thinking" to press Congress to advance their clients' agenda. And schools of political science and business at universities endowed by these same global interests train the next generation of leaders in their way of thinking.

These think tanks and universities serve as revolving doors for once and future government officials who will dutifully prioritize the imperatives of "the global economy."

The globalist ideology has even penetrated the Pentagon, the outfit established to defend America. Procurement officials have abandoned the Buy American mandates once required by law. They now go overseas to purchase parts, technology, and supplies for our weapons systems and troops. These officials, many of them high-ranking military officers, then pass through the revolving door to well-paid positions in global corporations supplying the Defense Department.

The Architecture of a Global Governing Structure

With the Treaty of Rome and a catalogue of free trade agreements, the transnational technocrats set out to make a borderless world a reality. Over the decades, Washington outsourced its decision- and policymaking to international organizations such as the World Trade Organization (WTO), the International Monetary Fund, and the World Bank.

Strobe Talbott described these institutions as "protominis- tries of trade, finance, and development for a united world." They are part of "the postwar international rules-based order" that our State Department promotes every day. When the WTO set trade policy for the U.S. and the world, its goal was an "efficient" global economy, not a higher living standard for Americans.

In the same way the WTO ran America's economic policy, the Paris climate accord would have run energy and environmental policy for the U.S. Whether or not you believe the stated goals of these deals are laudable, the problem remains that the dictates of these globalist institutions are beyond review by our elected representatives.

Now, the Chinese Communist Party has been welcomed into these institutions, and it is using globalization as a Trojan horse to take over the world. It has control of the World Bank, the World Health Organization (WHO), and more than a dozen U.N. agencies.

The CCP portrays itself as the defender of globalization, when its true agenda is "globalism for you, nationalism for us."

China flouts the rules of the WTO even as it calls on other nations to cede decision-making power to that organization.

The Wuhan virus pandemic has laid bare the dangers of globalism for all to see. Outsourcing our manufacturing power to communist China left us dependent on that totalitarian regime for medical supplies and other essential goods.

Outsourcing our political decision-making to transnational agencies, from the WHO to the WTO, puts us at the mercy of whoever controls those institutions.

Everyone has woken up to the dangers—well, just about everyone.

You'll still hear some insist we must "collaborate with Beijing" to solve the world's problems.

They don't understand: the regime in Beijing *is* the world's problem.

CHAPTER IV

How China Buys Influence

The American people know our relationship with the communist government of China has been dysfunctional, destructive, and must change.

Yet the "experts" and leaders keep telling us what they've been telling us for years: Nothing to worry about. We must "collaborate" with Beijing on the problems facing the world, whether it's climate change or the pandemic.

Why is it they can't see what is so clear to the rest us: the CCP is the problem.

It's not an accident or a coincidence that the policies these leaders of culture, business, and politics advocate benefit the CCP.

The Chinese Communist Party is waging information warfare to shape American public opinion and influence our economic and government policies to benefit the Beijing regime.

The CCP doesn't shape public opinion by buying billboards and TV ads.

They buy entire companies and co-opt our leaders!

Its methods are more sophisticated and insidious than paying American agents of influence with envelopes stuffed with cash. Usually, the agents don't even know they've been recruited.

The CCP manipulates the self-interest of its targets to make them its unwitting agents.

Rarely do you hear one of these agents of influence say, "I've thought about and you know what, that Communist Party of China is great—we oughta let it run the show! Everyone get on board!"

Instead, they'll say something along the lines of "doing business with the CCP is good ol' free market capitalism," or "we need a peaceful and harmonious world," or "this is what any reasonable person would advocate."

But everything they say and do—or don't say and don't do—advances the aims of the CCP.

These agents of influence fall roughly into four categories, and Beijing plays each accordingly.

Four Ways to Become an Influencer

The Vested

These influencers have a vested interest in continuing the status quo. Their fortunes derive from commerce with China.

In this category you will find the owners of our major media companies: Disney, the parent of ABC News, owns a theme park and distributes films in the People's Republic. Ditto for NBC (Universal theme park/studio), CBS (Paramount studio) and CNN (Warner Brothers theme park/studio).

Hollywood needs permission from China's government to distribute its movies, so it gives the CCP "final cut"—it lets the communist censors choose what you and I see on screens in this country. You will not see a major Hollywood film portraying China's communist government as the brutal dictatorship it is.

The CCP leveraged the National Basketball Association's business in China to silence any criticism from the high-profile athletes who are role models to many.

As Washington was negotiating a trade deal with Beijing, the CCP leadership told American executives in China to lobby Washington to remove the tariffs the administration had imposed. They didn't say "or else." But the message wasn't lost.

For decades, American businesses in China wouldn't speak up, even when the CCP hacked their computers, stole blueprints, and produced knockoffs of their own products. Not only did they not file complaints against trade law violations, they went further and advocated for continuing the same lopsided dysfunctional relationship that has empowered Beijing. They feared offending the regime that had absolute control over their business in China, that could withhold or revoke permits, impose restrictions, and even confiscate their factories.

This is how American businesses became Beijing's apologists and lobbyists.

In this category of the vested you will find Wall Street financiers who earn billions from doing business with China's communist government. Beijing has given billions to Bridgewater Associates, a private equity fund run by Ray Dalio. You will see Dalio on TV telling us all how China's communist system is superior to our own.

Another example: Hank Paulson, who headed Goldman Sachs when he wasn't U.S. Treasury secretary. He and his fellow Wall Street bankers have been reliable partners in advancing the CCP line promoting globalism *über alles*. Wall Street is in it for

the money, and they either don't realize or don't care they're selling out the United States. Commerce has weakened their spirit
of patriotism.

Wall Street has pushed hard to invest American pension and
index funds in Chinese government-controlled companies. This
not only shovels money to the dictators, it threatens to turn millions of Americans into Beijing agents of influence, as they will
be loathe to stand up to the CCP lest their stock portfolios be
endangered.

Among the vested: Beijing has directly paid McKinsey &
Company management consultants, and McKinsey in turn tells
its clients, including top companies and politicians, what a great
and responsible business partner the CCP is.

Then there's the import lobby. Everyone from Wal-Mart to
the American Apparel & Footwear Association (really the footwear and apparel *importers* association), to the U.S. Chamber
of Commerce and the Business Roundtable depend on cheap
imports from China. They lobby against tariffs on China, which
is, coincidentally, exactly what the CCP wants. Note that many
newspapers depend on advertising revenue from these importers
and the retailers who carry their goods.

When these vested interests say it's in "the national interest"
for us to continue down the current road with China, they mean
it's in their own business interest.

The Chinese Communist Party understands the corrupting
influence of foreign business entanglements. Financial journalist
and author Eamonn Fingleton explains how the Chinese empire
threw itself open to foreign capital in the nineteenth century.

"The foreign investors formed alliances with the local elites,
who in effect became lobbyists for the foreign capital. Foreign
money quickly suffused government and largely disabled

independent policy-making. Soon the local elites came to identify with the foreigners," he writes.

The CCP learned from history and now runs the same play, only in the other direction. It bought American elites and uses them as its lobbyists in Washington. The elites have come to identify their interests with the CCP's interests.

The CCP uses this same tactic around the world.

Germany, France, Great Britain—all have global corporations eager to drink from the river of CCP money. The European Union was silent when Beijing reneged on a treaty and cracked down on Hong Kong.

Diplomats in Brussels and other European capitals took their cue from corporations that didn't want anything to get in the way of doing business with Beijing.

Remember that the next time you hear "we can't go it alone, we have to work with our allies" to confront the CCP.

The Weak

They *cannot* see the danger. They are slaves to fear. They fear war and any kind of conflict. They will say "the era of competition between nations is past," "this is not a zero-sum game," "we can have a win-win deal with Beijing." Their immediate fear prevents them from seeing the bigger picture.

The Prejudiced

They *will not* see the danger. Their minds are made up.

Some are prejudiced by their absolute faith in the infallibility of their Ivy League alma maters where professors taught them how the world (allegedly) works. Their prestigious degrees gave them prestigious careers and made them experts but bound them fast to conventional wisdom. Harry Truman said an expert was "a fella who was afraid to learn anything new because then he wouldn't be an expert anymore."

Others have such a deep loathing of a former president whom they disagree with on every issue that they are incapable of evaluating the CCP issue dispassionately. If the much-loathed former president is against it, they will reflexively take the opposite view, or dismiss it. Journalists and pundits who claim the former president's criticism of the CCP is an effort to deflect criticism fall into this camp.

The "Moderates"

These "reasonable" men and women think better of China's government than it deserves. They are perhaps the most dangerous.

They were educated at Harvard and Yale, served as high-ranking officials in Washington, belong to the Council on Foreign Relations, and write for prestigious journals.

They all know each other, go to the same cocktail parties, and go through the revolving doors that whirl between Wall Street, Washington, universities, and think tanks.

Think tanks—those high-sounding institutions turning out policy papers and pronouncements on issues of global and national importance—are another instrument Beijing uses to spread its influence.

These organizations are not required to disclose foreign sources of funding, and even if they did, it wouldn't necessarily tell the whole story. Beijing funnels money through a shell game of outfits—law firms, lobbyists, individuals, private companies, and nonprofits with pleasant-sounding names.

This money ends up in think tanks, where the staff of moderate men and women are careful not to offend donors who have business interests in China and not to depart from the pro-Beijing consensus view.

These moderate men turn out "neutral," "authoritative" studies and op-eds advocating "moderate" policies for politicians to stay the course with Beijing.

Universities for Sale

Chinese students represent the largest cohort of foreign students in the United States today, and they pay higher tuition than American students.

The CCP leverages this money flow to compromise our universities.

Universities, like other businesses, don't want to bite the hand that feeds them. They tailor their curriculum and extracurricular activities—such as speakers invited on campus—to avoid "sensitive topics," including Tibet, Hong Kong, and the CCP's numerous other human rights abuses.

The foreign students from China—whose visas are all approved by the Beijing government—press university administrators not to allow other students to discuss topics they claim would "offend" their heritage, by which they mean the CCP.

Sometimes the CCP is more direct in its methods of buying influence, literally paying professors at our leading institutions of higher learning. The FBI arrested Charles Lieber, the chair of Harvard's Chemistry and Chemical Biology Department, for accepting millions of dollars from the Wuhan virology lab and then lying about it.

Leiber is not alone. A UCLA professor was convicted of taking CCP money to illegally send semiconductors with military applications to China. A University of Kansas professor hid the fact he was working full time for a Chinese university while he was conducting federally funded research here. One of the top researchers at the University of Texas MD Anderson Cancer Center didn't reveal he was also being paid $14 million by a cancer institute in China.

The payoff for Beijing from these operations is twofold. Besides stealing research, the CCP is also buying influence in academia. These professors, particularly in the case of Harvard's Lieber, perpetuate the myth among colleagues and university administrators that communist China is a friend and trustworthy partner.

Along the myth-perpetuation line, the CCP has given large grants to American colleges to host Confucius Institutes. These CCP-controlled institutions are disguised as simply Chinese language and cultural education centers. In fact, they parrot the CCP line and promote a distorted, benign image of that brutal dictatorship. They are a crucial weapon in the information war the CCP is waging to normalize itself to the next generation of America's leaders.

In addition to buying professors and entire universities, the CCP uses students as spies.

China has a series of military universities, military students attending non-military universities, and departments at universities doing a lot of work for the military. They send these "students" to American universities, where they work on research projects funded by U.S. taxpayers and funnel the research back to Beijing. When law enforcement shuts down this espionage, the CCP and its unwitting accomplices in the American media cry "racism," claiming the spies are being singled out because of their race.

Using Campaign Donors to Influence Politicians

In the 1992 presidential campaign, candidate Bill Clinton slammed George H. W. Bush for coddling the "butchers of Beijing." He promised he would get tough and link trade relations to the CCP's human rights record.

After Clinton was elected, Beijing enlisted its allies in business and Wall Street to convince the new president to change course. This is another example of the classical Chinese military strategy of using influential advisers in your opponent's leadership circle to turn your opponent's house on itself.

In *The Hundred-Year Marathon: China's Secret Strategy to Replace America as the Global Superpower,*[12] Michael Pillsbury details "the Clinton coup." Beijing played Robert Rubin, then chairman of the National Economic Council; Harvard economist Larry Summers, then undersecretary of the Treasury; and other "free trade" acolytes in President Clinton's camp to persuade him to give China preferential access to our market and technology.

Beijing promised leading businessmen lucrative deals worth hundreds of millions of dollars. These big campaign donors lobbied the president, asking him to not do anything that would interfere with selling Boeing airliners or launching American satellites on Chinese rockets. Beijing used Clinton's own people to achieve its goal.

It worked. President Clinton abandoned his tough line. Like Bush and Carter and Ford before him, he expanded economic ties with China, believing it would turn the communist dictatorship into a free market social democracy.

The World Bank provided China's communist government with an economic strategy to catch up with the United States, while the U.S. government handed over sensitive technology, military know-how, intelligence, and expert advice. Wall Street prodded American companies to invest more and more in China.

A Senate investigation detailed[13] how the Chinese government covertly used political donations in 1996 to gain access and influence politicians at the local, state, and federal level. A high-ranking member of the Chinese People's Liberation Army even visited President Clinton and the First Lady for a photo op at the White House.

The Care and Feeding of Reporters

The CCP influences our media in several different ways. As noted above, many media companies have business interests inside China, making them susceptible to the CCP's extortion.

In addition, advertising supports much of our media. Many of the advertisers either import their products from China, or have interests in or with the People's Republic.

No one needs to come out and tell the president of the news division or entertainment division certain subjects are off-limits. But don't expect to see a series on undercover Chinese spies in America—it wouldn't find any sponsors, and everyone at the networks knows not to go there.

When it comes to shaping news, the CCP is adept at influencing reporters on the China beat.

Coverage of the trade negotiations shows how the Chinese Communist Party has used our news media, our financial system, and our political divisions to achieve its goals.

Here's how it works:

A Chinese official claiming to have "inside information" on the status of negotiations—namely, that American negotiators are ready to accept Beijing's demands—gives an American correspondent Beijing's approved narrative. The reporter passes it along to headquarters in New York, Washington, or London.

The newspaper, citing "anonymous sources close to the talks," then reports as "fact" what is nothing more than China's spin. U.S. negotiators who prefer to negotiate in secret decline to comment.

However, unnamed "administration officials" sympathetic to Wall Street hint that the proposal originating from Beijing is "being discussed."

Once in print, broadcast media and others in the financial and political press pick up the story, further amplifying the spin China planted.

At this stage, the media ask the administration's economic advisers to respond to the "news," cementing the narrative made in China.

Then reliably pro-Beijing Wall Street and U.S. Chamber of Commerce mouthpieces weigh in, not surprisingly declaring the national interest and the upward movement of the Dow require that we immediately adopt the proposal originally floated by the CCP.

The CCP has expertly used Wall Street and the media to advance the line that the health of the American economy depends on Washington making a deal, any deal, with China as soon as possible—if not sooner.

The fact is, our economy remained strong without a deal and inflation was flat, defying the tariff-hating doomsayers. The "tariffs must go" line played to the interests of the vested (and the reporters who cover them), the conflict-avoidance predisposition of the weak, the reflexive tendencies of the prejudiced, and the "reasonableness" of the moderates.

Corrupting Everything It Touches

In targeting influential individuals and institutions in America, the CCP uses the weaknesses of its targets against them. Businessmen like money, so it offers lucrative commercial opportunities. Politicians need money, so it uses campaign donors to work its will on our political leaders. Policymakers believe they are big thinkers and strategic masterminds, so the CCP cloaks its nationalist agenda in the language of "globalization," globalism," and "a post-national future." Reporters succumb to groupthink, they self-censor and suck up to their powerful sources on Wall Street and in Washington, so the CCP plays off these weaknesses.

The Foreign Agents Registration Act (FARA) requires those doing the bidding of a foreign government to register with the federal government or risk five years in prison. But the law is outdated.

The Chinese Communist Party employs the classical Chinese military strategy of "turn your opponent's house on itself" in its information and its economic warfare.

The CCP's sophisticated approach has created an army of unregistered foreign agents inside the U.S.

We must update the registration act to deal with the new threat.

The CCP corrupts everything and everyone it touches—in our universities, our businesses, our culture, and our government.

CHAPTER V

The American System—The Origin of America's Prosperity

For most of her history, America was guided by a devotion to what would raise the standard of living for her citizens, a self-governing people proud to be self-reliant.

It was considered the American way for the citizens of this country to make the goods sold in this country.

The ideologies of globalism and free trade are foreign imports.

Today, we hear "experts" say Americans benefit from cheap imports, and "cheap" should outweigh all other considerations.

But is that true?

Should ready access to cheaper imported goods be the goal of our foreign trade policy, indeed of our entire economic policy? Is that the best way to raise our nation's standard of living?

These questions have been debated throughout our nation's history.

The founders answered resoundingly, "No."

The founders were not free traders. The American Revolution was a rebellion against globalism, and in many respects, it was a trade war.

The Boston Tea Party was a response to cheap imports.

The British East India Company priced its tea to be cheaper than the colonial merchants' tea. King George's prime minister Lord North believed price would convince Americans to buy British because, as North said,[14] "men will always go to the cheapest markets."

Americans said no, and the Sons of Liberty tossed the British tea into Boston Harbor.

The king forbade colonists from producing textiles, furnishings, and metal goods instead of purchasing them from Britain. This irritated enterprising Yankees.

National pride and the desire for self-governance drove the founders to draft the Declaration of Independence and wage the War of Independence from Great Britain.

And the independence for which they fought was economic as well as political.

The founders of our nation firmly believed cheaper imports from Britain should not be allowed to drive American producers out of business.

The founders knew their new nation would not be truly independent if we relied on finished goods from Great Britain, then "the workshop of the world."

President Washington was committed to developing industry on our own shores.

"A free people...should promote such manufactories as tend to render them independent from others for essential, particularly military supplies," George Washington declared in his first address to Congress.

The new national government didn't leave the task to chance. It took deliberate and specific steps to ensure Americans would produce the goods we needed to thrive. President Washington's treasury secretary, Alexander Hamilton, was a fierce proponent of import duties, or tariffs.

The second bill passed by Congress and signed by Washington placed a tariff on imported goods.

Hamilton designed economic development policies that were distinctly different than the British system of "free trade." Hamilton's plan came to be known as the American System.

What Is the American System?

The founders understood that America could not be independent and strong if we relied on other nations for our manufactured goods. They understood the United States had the natural resources, the technology, the labor force, and ample customers at home to support domestic industry and be largely self-sufficient.

As an example to his countrymen to Buy American, George Washington wore a suit of American-made cloth at his inauguration in 1789.

"I hope it will not be a great while before it will be unfashionable for a gentleman to appear in any other dress. Indeed, we have already been too long subject to British prejudices," he wrote.

Washington believed the United States could manufacture as well as farm, and he instructed Treasury Secretary Alexander Hamilton to come up with a plan to develop industry on these shores.

Hamilton's plan, detailed in his 1791 *Report on the Subject of Manufactures*, called for tariffs that would raise revenues and protect infant American industries against predatory competition, and government procurement contracts to encourage American manufacturers.

The American System, also called the American School of economics, guided U.S. national economic development from the earliest days of the republic, through the Civil War, and into the better part of the twentieth century. It built the United States from an agrarian frontier society into the world's largest economy and greatest industrial power.

The American System had three basic tenets to promote domestic industry. The government would

1. use tariffs to discourage imports, and leverage the purchasing power of government to give preference to domestic producers;
2. invest in roads, ports, dams, canals, and turnpikes—then called "internal improvements," now called infrastructure—to facilitate commerce; and
3. regulate credit to spur economic development and deter speculation.

Congress passed the Tariff Act of 1789 as its second piece of legislation. The opening section reads, "It is necessary for the support of the government, the discharge of the debts of the United States, and for the encouragement and protection of manufactures that a duty be laid on goods and merchandise imported."

The tax on imports raised revenue to fund the government and prevented foreign goods from smothering our own infant industries. Tariffs were the nation's primary source of revenue for its first 150 years. Consider: we taxed foreign industries, not our own.

In 1791, Treasury Secretary Alexander Hamilton delivered his *Report on the Subject of Manufactures* to President Washington. It laid out the plan for the federal government to nurture the growth of domestic manufacturing industries in the United States rather than allow the new nation to depend on manufactured goods from abroad.

Hamilton declared: "Not only the wealth; the independence and security of a Country, appear to be materially connected with the prosperity of manufactures. Every nation…ought to endeavor to possess within itself all the essentials of national supply. These comprise the means to Subsistence habitation clothing and defence."

A diversified economy of agriculture, merchants, and manufacturing would provide opportunities for Americans of all skills, "furnishing greater scope for the diversity of talents and dispositions which discriminate men from each other," Hamilton wrote.

Hamilton's report stood in contrast to "free traders" who believed America should confine itself to farming, export raw materials, and buy manufactured goods from Great Britain.

Thomas Jefferson Has a Change of Heart

At first, Thomas Jefferson was one of those free traders. He opposed developing American industry. Jefferson envisioned a purely agricultural economy that would "let the work-shops" remain in Europe.

But Jefferson had a change of heart, writing in 1809:[15]

> My idea is that we should encourage home man-
> ufactures to the extent of our own consumption
> of everything of which we raise the raw material.
> I do not think it fair [of] the ship-owners to say
> we ought not to make our own axes, nails, &c.,

here, that they may have the benefit of carrying the iron to Europe, and bringing back the axes, nails, &c.

Shorter version: if we can make here, we should make it here.

The War of 1812 cemented Jefferson's commitment to economic nationalism.

The war began as a trade dispute. Britannia ruled the waves, and its navy embargoed "those necessaries for which we have permitted ourselves to be dependent on others, even…clothing," as he put it. British rockets inspired the lyrics to our national anthem, British forces burned the White House, and British free trade fired Jefferson's commitment to tariffs and American national self-sufficiency. He wrote in 1815,[16]

> The prohibiting duties [tariffs] we lay on all articles of foreign manufacture which prudence requires us to establish at home, with the patriotic determination of every good citizen to use no foreign article which can be made within ourselves without regard to difference of price, secures us against a relapse into foreign dependency.

Jefferson explicitly renounced his earlier belief that America should be a strictly agrarian nation that depended on England "for manufactures." He went out of his way to disabuse Benjamin Austin[17] of that notion in 1816, writing:

> *To be independent for the comforts of life we must fabricate them ourselves. We must now place the manufacturer by the side of the agriculturist....* Shall we make our own comforts, or go without

them, at the will of a foreign nation? He, therefore, who is now against domestic manufacture,
must be for reducing us either to dependence
on that foreign nation, or to be clothed in skins,
and to live like wild beasts in dens and caverns.
I am not one of these; experience has taught me
that manufactures are now as necessary to our
independence as to our comfort; *and if those who
quote me as of a different opinion, will keep pace
with me in purchasing nothing foreign where an
equivalent of domestic fabric*[ation] *can be ob-
tained, without regard to difference of price*, it
will not be our fault if we do not soon have a
supply at home equal to our demand, and wrest
the weapon of distress from the hand which has
wielded it. [Emphasis added]

Notice that Jefferson encouraged buying the American goods
"without regard to difference in price"—that is, even if the imports were cheaper. "Cheap" and "cheaper" did not enter in the
patriot's thinking.

The most famous and influential advocate of the American
System was Henry Clay of Kentucky. He served as Speaker of the
House and later as a senator.

Clay's famous "American System" speech from 1824 describes
America's current crisis—and the solution:

Poverty befalls any nation that neglects and
abandons the care of its own industry, leaving it
exposed to the action of foreign powers. There is a
remedy, and that consists in adopting a Genuine

American System accomplished by the establishment of a tariff—with the view of promoting
American industry—the cause is the cause of the
country, and it must and it will prevail.

Abraham Lincoln: When We Buy American, We Get the Goods and the Money

Abraham Lincoln was Henry Clay's acolyte and a firm believer in
the Genuine American System. "Give us a protective tariff and we
will have the greatest country on earth," Lincoln declared while
campaigning for Henry Clay in 1844.

Congressman Lincoln argued, "Abandonment of the protective policy by the American Government must result in the
increase of both useless labour, and idleness [unemployment]; and
so, in proportion must produce want and ruin among our people."
Unemployment, want, and ruin were concerns then as now.

Lincoln ran on a platform of "protection [tariffs], homesteads
[free Western land], rivers and harbors [internal improvements],
and the Pacific railroad." The industrial states of the North handed
him the presidency.

For building the transcontinental railroad, Lincoln insisted
American steel be used even though British rails were cheaper.
"When we buy manufactured goods abroad, we get the goods and
the foreigner gets the money. When we buy the manufactured
goods at home, we get both the goods and the money," said Abe.
More honest words have never been spoken.

Lincoln's economic policy was driven by the conviction that
production has primacy over consumption. Producing more en-
ables one to consume more—that's how to raise the American
standard of living.

Workers who produce more earn more and spend more. Consumption would rise in tandem with production and earning. Build it and they will come.

"Every man is a consumer to the whole extent of his production. To that point he will go, and beyond it he cannot go," wrote Henry Carey,[18] Lincoln's economic adviser. By earning (producing) more, one is able to consume (buy) more. Producing always comes first.

Rather than seeking cheaper goods, the goal[19] is "to produce dear labour, that is, high-priced and valuable labour," Carey wrote.

"Cheap Is the Badge of Poverty"

William McKinley was another champion of the American System and would become the twenty-fifth president of the United States in 1896. As chairman of the House Ways and Means Committee, he fathered the tariff that bore his name. The philosophy behind the McKinley Tariff was simple. McKinley believed a foreign manufacturer had

> no right or claim to equality with our own. He is not amenable to our laws.… He pays no taxes. He performs no civil duties.… He contributes nothing to the support, the progress, and glory of the nation. Free foreign trade…results in giving our money, our manufactures, and our markets to other nations, to the injury of our labor, our tradespeople and our farmers.

If American industry has to pay taxes and the costs of our labor, health, and environmental laws, it only makes sense that

foreign manufacturers should bear a similar burden if they want
to sell on our shores.

McKinley's warning from two centuries ago rings true today. Change "Europe" to "Asia" and these ring as the words of
a prophet:

> This country will not and can not prosper under
> any system that does not recognize the differ-
> ence of conditions in Europe and America. Open
> competition between high-paid American labor
> and poorly paid European labor will either drive
> out of existence American industry or lower
> American wages.

In 1889, McKinley also had an answer for those who say cheap
imports are good for America:

> They say "everything would be so cheap" if we
> only had free trade. Well, everything would be
> cheap and everybody would be cheap. I do not
> prize the word "cheap."... It is the badge of pov-
> erty...when things were the cheapest, men were the
> poorest.... Cheap? Why, cheap merchandise means
> cheap men, and cheap men mean a cheap country;
> and that is not the kind of Government our fathers
> founded.... We want labor to be well paid, we want
> the products of the farm...we want everything we
> make and produce to pay a fair compensation to
> the producer. That is what makes good times.[20]

"A fair compensation to the producer"—take care of the producer and the rest will take care of itself.

The man who succeeded McKinley in the White House, Teddy Roosevelt, declared, "Thank God I am not a free trader." He understood how tariffs "will equalize the cost of production here and abroad; that is, will equalize the cost of labor here and abroad."

In the decades Washington, D.C., pursued the American System, from 1860s to the first decade of the twentieth century, America's gross national product quadrupled. U.S. coal production rose by 800 percent, steel rails by 523 percent, railroad track mileage by 567 percent, and wheat production by 256 percent.

We surpassed Britain as the world's major industrial power, with output rising four times, from half of Britain's to more than double.

Following the path set by Washington, Hamilton, Clay, and Lincoln, America grew from an agrarian outpost to the greatest industrial power in world history in a century.

It was not a coincidence we had the highest tariff rates in history at the same time we saw the greatest economic expansion in history. Meanwhile, Europe and the Third World stagnated under free trade.

"A People Who Cannot Supply Their Own Demand Are Not Independent"

The goal of the patriots who built this country was political and economic independence.

William "Pig Iron" Kelley, a congressman from Philadelphia and chairman of the powerful tax-writing committee, believed iron and steel were the muscles of modern civilization. He understood economic and political independence are connected. "A people who cannot supply their own demand for iron and steel but

purchase it from foreigners beyond seas, are not independent...
they are politically dependent."

These patriots likened their cause to war, economic war, defending America against enemies with "missiles launched from their far-distant mines, mills, and factories," an attack that has "broken up industries as effectually as if the conquest had been effected by warlike weapons," Kelley declared.

The American System aims at delivering a higher standard of living for Americans—higher wages for workers, fair compensation for producers—rather than lower prices for consumers because *the consumer is the producer*—and must first be a producer.

Americans would find gainful employment producing the goods they consumed. It was a virtuous cycle, with "consuming" (buying) recycling wealth into the pockets of the "consumers," who were, importantly, producers of the goods as well. Americans made what they bought and bought what they made.

But toward the middle of the last century, under both Democratic and Republican administrations, the United States government increasingly abandoned the American System, the economic policies that built us into the greatest industrial power on earth.

The pursuit of global free trade brought about the collapse of American industries and wages as the U.S. imported more and more of the goods we had produced ourselves. The loss of revenue from bankrupted industries and Americans either unemployed or forced into lower-paying service jobs created yawning budget deficits at the municipal, state, and federal levels.

The good news is we can revive the virtuous cycle that resulted in the broad-based prosperity the world envied. We can make what we buy.

We don't have to be dependent on others. We have the resources and the talent to fabricate "the comforts of life" ourselves.

And we have the will.

We must once again declare our independence. Two hundred forty-seven years ago, Great Britain was waging economic war against us. Today, it is communist China.

The course of independence, national self-sufficiency, would be good for us, and good for the world.

Henry Carey wrote two centuries ago,

> To raise the value of labor throughout the world, we need only to raise the value of our own.... To diffuse intelligence and to promote the cause of morality throughout the world, we are required only to pursue the course that shall diffuse education throughout our own land, and shall enable every man more readily to acquire property, and with it respect for the rights of property."[21]

CHAPTER VI

Setting the Record Straight on Adam Smith

The ideology of "global free trade" has stripped our land of industry, destroyed the middle class, and weakened our nation. Its defenders claim globalism is the free market at work, as American as apple pie. They are wrong. The ideology of global free trade is not American nor is it the free market system.

In 1776, Adam Smith published *The Wealth of Nations*, his foundational economic treatise on the principles of the free market system. Contrary to what so many today mistakenly believe and claim, Smith did not argue for a world without nations or a world where corporate interests came before national interests. Smith wrote about increasing the wealth of *nations*, not the wealth of transnational corporations or the wealth of "the global economy."

Smith was an economic nationalist. He was a Britain First man. He put national interests first. He supported laws that required trade with Britain be done exclusively on British ships.

He believed nations should import what couldn't be produced at home and export the surplus that wasn't consumed at home.

Today, those who oppose tariffs on imports from China often invoke Adam Smith to justify their position. They really should know better. After all, Adam Smith would approve of the tariffs.

How do we know? He said so. Let's go to his own words.

Adam Smith's Guide to Tariffs

In *The Wealth of Nations*[22] Adam Smith describes the circumstances when a nation should impose tariffs and restrict imports, when, as he wrote, it would be "advantageous to lay some burden upon foreign [imports], for the encouragement of domestic industry." Notice he explicitly says he wants to encourage domestic industry—he makes a distinction between his nation's industry and those of *another nation*. He is not writing about a global economy without distinction among nations.

First, Smith said tariffs are justified to protect industries "necessary for the defense of the country."

The defense of Great Britain, for example, depends very much upon the number of its sailors and shipping. The act of navigation, therefore, very properly endeavors to give the sailors and shipping of Great Britain the monopoly on the trade of their own country, in some cases by absolute prohibitions, and in others by heavy burdens upon the shipping of foreign countries.

Smith believed the defense of Great Britain justified a monopoly on shipping and trade. Therefore, he supported the Act of Navigation and Trade, which kept foreign ships out of British ports. (This would become a flash point with the North American colonies that led to the establishment of a new American nation.)

America until recently depended on Russia to launch our spy satellites, and China still produces electronics for our jet fighters. Foreign competitors enjoying subsidies from their governments and duty-free access to our market have decimated our own space launch and electronics industries. Adam Smith would not approve of our national government standing idly by and allowing this to happen.

Another case, Smith wrote, "in which it will generally be advantageous to lay some burden upon foreign imports for the encouragement of domestic industry, is, when some tax is imposed on the [domestic industry.] In this case, it seems reasonable that an equal tax [i.e., tariff] should be imposed" on the foreign imports.

Minimum wage laws, environmental and workplace safety regulations, and Social Security and Medicare costs are examples of taxes[23] imposed on American industry. Their costs are reflected in the price of goods produced in the U.S. According to Smith's doctrine, "an equal tax should be imposed upon" imports to level the playing field for American producers.

Another of those occasions for which Smith advocates tariffs is when

> Some foreign nation [may restrain] by high duties or prohibitions the importation of some of our manufactures into their country. Revenge in this case naturally dictates retaliation, and that we should impose the like duties and prohibitions upon the importation of some or all of their manufactures into ours.

For decades, China has slapped stiff tariffs on American imports to keep them out while we let their goods pass through our ports practically duty-free. In situations like this, Adam Smith advises it's wise to impose similarly high tariffs because "retaliations of this kind...will procure the repeal of the high duties" placed on our own exports. To do less would amount to unilateral disarmament in the economic war China is waging against America.

Finally, Smith understood that the purpose of trade is to increase the wealth of the nation and benefit its people. Any theory of trade is worthwhile only so far as it advances the well-being of real people living in the real world. The economy must serve man, not the other way around.

In this spirit he wrote, "Humanity may require" import tariffs to be reduced gradually, "and with a good deal of reserve and circumspection. Were those high duties and prohibitions taken away all at once, cheaper foreign goods of the same kind might be poured so fast into the home market, as to deprive all at once many thousands of our people of their ordinary employment and means of subsistence."

What he wrote three centuries ago we see today. A flood of "cheaper foreign" imports of the clothing we wear, the TVs we watch, the cars we drive, the machines we work on, and the toys our children play with "poured so fast" into our land that Americans who once produced "goods of the same kind," with their own hands, have been deprived of their "employment and means of subsistence." Indeed, this flood has swept many Americans into a valley of death, deprivation, and poverty.

Adam Smith would not approve of the "open borders at whatever cost" course our nation has been on. In fact, he would regard the free trade absolutists of today as delusional. "To expect...that freedom of trade should ever be entirely restored in Great Britain is as absurd as to expect that an Oceana or a Utopia should ever be established in it," Smith wrote.

Smith: Give Money and Jobs to the Greatest Number of Your Country's People

Today's evangelists of globalism and free trade also rely on a selective reading—actually, a misreading—of another classic economic text to justify the outsourcing of our industries to places like communist China.

They point to David Ricardo's treatise from 1817 in which he laid out the theory of "comparative advantage" in international trade, *On the Principles of Political Economy and Taxation.*[24]

Ricardo calls for an international division of labor, with countries specializing in those particular goods they are best at making and trading with other countries for other goods, rather than making everything at home. He uses the example of Portugal trading Madeira wine for British textiles.

But today's free-trade-*über-alles* lobby ignores the important premise underlying Ricardo's theory: he assumes capital will not cross *national* borders; it will stay in its *country of origin.*

That, of course, is not what's happening today. Global corporations and financiers move assets and capital around the globe in nanoseconds with a keystroke.

In his famous treatise, Ricardo explains the crucial caveat to his theory:

> The fancied or real insecurity of capital, when not under the immediate control of its owner, together with the natural disinclination which every man has to quit the country of his birth

and connexions, and intrust himself with all his
habits fixed, to a strange government and new
laws, check the emigration of capital.

In plain English, he's saying no one will sink their capital in a
foreign country ruled by "a strange government and new laws" for
the same reason they won't leave family, friends, and their native
country behind to live in a foreign country. They're not comfortable entrusting their lives and fortunes to strangers.

On this point, he and Adam Smith agreed. Smith said a businessman will "employ his capital as near home as he can" so he
can keep an eye on it. "He can know better the character and situation of the persons whom he trusts, and if he should happen to
be deceived, he knows better the laws of the country from which
he must seek redress."

Thus "every individual naturally inclines to employ his capital
in the manner in which it is likely to afford the greatest support
to domestic industry, and to give revenue and employment to the
greatest number of people of his own country."

Smith thought this inclination to invest in one's own country
was a positive thing, not a shortcoming. He cited it as an example
of how an "invisible hand" works to promote a broader good:

> By preferring the support of domestic to that of
> foreign industry, he intends only his own secu-
> rity...he is in this, as in many other cases, led
> by an invisible hand to promote an end which
> was no part of his intention.... By pursuing his
> own interest, he frequently promotes that of
> the society.

Ricardo also recognized "men of property" would be "satisfied with a low rate of profits in their own country, rather than seek" higher profits "in foreign nations."

And he too didn't see this as a negative, the symptom of weak sentimentality or lack of steely nerves. To the contrary, Ricardo said he'd "be sorry to see weakened" this natural affinity to one's country.

That's quite different than today's business leaders who forget America and couldn't care less about their fellow Americans. These executives see themselves as too sophisticated for "nostalgic nationalism" and dream of a fully integrated global economy efficiently combining the resources of country X with the labor of country Y to serve markets in country Z, free of "restrictions imposed by individual national governments," as Wall Street banker and former State Department official George Ball told Congress in 1967.

This ideology of globalism has nothing in common with the economic nationalism of Adam Smith, nor does the regime in Beijing adhere to the principles of the free market system.

David Ricardo and Adam Smith counseled capitalists to avoid investing in "a strange government" lest they "happen to be deceived."

Today's captains of industry and finance ignored that advice and gambled their capital, their enterprises, and the future of our nation on a totalitarian regime. And deceived they were.

They thought the World Trade Organization could save them, but they were wrong. The CCP lies, cheats, steals, and violates every promise it makes, including those it makes to the WTO.

Instead of following fanciful theories of "free trade," we'd do better to stick to the system of free markets and economic nationalism taught by Adam Smith.

CHAPTER VII

Tearing Down "The House of World Order"

The coronavirus pandemic exposed how badly the post-World War II "international rules-based order" needs renovation.

This "international rules-based order" is a euphemism for globalism—and globalism took a beating from the microbe.

The pandemic showed that the true cost of the China price is very high indeed. It showed how an economy reliant on global supply chains and just-in-time inventory management is fragile.

And it showed how the Chinese Communist Party is not the benign force we expected it to be when we welcomed China into "the family of trading nations."

The CCP follows the Marxist-Leninist ideology of a communist "dictatorship of the proletariat," or working class, led by the "vanguard party," the CCP. In the People's Republic of China, the purpose of society and the economy is to support the power of the party.

The Chinese Communist Party holds absolute power in China. The party and the government are indistinguishable. The CCP's power and influence reach into every corner of the state, society, and economy. It commands the government, courts, military, media, education, and business. No organization is independent; all answer to the chairman of the Chinese Communist Party.

The individual has no rights, such as freedom of speech, freedom of the press, or freedom of assembly; the individual exists solely to serve the state, the collective good as the party defines it. Private property does not exist; the party/state controls that as well.

The CCP believes its system of monopolistic control of all economic, political, and social activity is superior to all other forms of government. As a Leninist party, it is expansionist. It believes imposing "socialism with Chinese characteristics" on the world is both its responsibility and a historical inevitability.

Those who hoped giving the CCP Western technology and capital would lead it to reform were blind. The CCP cannot abandon its core beliefs without abandoning its reason to exist.

Rather than reforming the CCP, we ended up strengthening it.

The pandemic exposed all the cracks in the globalization project the elites have been pursuing for the past seventy years.

The World Trade Organization is a cornerstone of that project, and like the World Health Organization, its sister in the globalist pantheon, the WTO is under increasing pressure.

"The global economic system as we know it is a relic; it requires reform, top to bottom. We should begin with one of its leading institutions, the World Trade Organization. We should abolish it," Senator Josh Hawley wrote in the *New York Times*.[25]

True. The WTO is one product that has outlived its sell-by date.

Outsourcing Our Government, Outsourcing Our Industry

The World Trade Organization was born in the heady days after the Berlin Wall fell. Gone were the days when Western industrial democracies, the free world, stood shoulder to shoulder in a trade and military alliance against the communist bloc. In the new post-Cold War era after the wall came down, goods and capital would move freely in a global economy, establishing universal peace, prosperity, and democracy. It was, the thinking went, the end of history.

The WTO was born in 1995, but its conception dates further back, to 1947, when the State Department sought to create an International Trade Organization "to bring about world peace... and prevent World War III."

A California congressman at the time described Washington's negotiators as "boatloads of smug diplomats, all-wise economists, experts, theorists, specialists, and whatnots eager to barter away the little factory in Wichita, the little shop in Keokuk."

The negotiators failed in '47, but Washington kept the dream alive over the decades. "What's good for the global economy" replaced "what's good for America" as the guiding principle for Washington's policymakers, diplomats, and strategists.

The "experts" went about implementing their plan without debate or congressional vote. It was not an oversight that no one came right out and told the American people we were replacing our nation and system of government with something new.

Richard Gardner, a respected diplomat who was Bill Clinton's ambassador to Spain, explained the game: "The 'house of world order' will have to be built from the bottom up.... An end run about national sovereignty, eroding it piece by piece, will accomplish much more than a frontal assault."[26]

Strobe Talbott served in Bill Clinton's State Department when the WTO was founded. He described "The Birth of the Global Nation" in *Time* magazine in 1992: "Countries are…artificial and temporary…. Within the next hundred years…nationhood as we know it will be obsolete; all states will recognize a single, global authority. A phrase briefly fashionable in the mid-20th century—"citizen of the world"—will have assumed real meaning by the end of the 21st."

Today, NBC and ABC promote the "Global Citizen Festival" on national television. CNN, on its New Year's Eve broadcast, has replaced "Auld Lang Syne" with "Imagine," John Lennon's ode to a world without borders, countries or religions, helping us to forget an old acquaintance with our country and culture.

The WTO: An Organization That Doesn't Follow Its Own Rules

Long before the pandemic exposed the follies and fallacies of the globalist project, before it showed us how other nations will always put their own interests first when push comes to shove, administrations on both sides of the aisle had problems with the World Trade Organization.

One of those problems involves the organization's Appellate Body, the judges who interpret WTO rules and settle disputes among members over unfair trade practices. The problem is that the WTO doesn't follow its own rules.

Article 17.5 of WTO rules[27] says cases must be settled within ninety days. In reality, cases drag on for years[28] during which time the victims go bankrupt while awaiting justice.

The rules also say judges cannot be affiliated with any government. Yet in a recent case[29] involving paper imports, none of the judges met the WTO's criteria, and one was actually an official of the Chinese government. The judges, not surprisingly, ruled against the U.S.

U.S. Trade Representative (USTR) Robert Lighthizer blasted the ruling as "the latest example of judicial activism"[30] by the WTO aimed at undermining U.S. trade laws.

And when the WTO isn't flouting its own rules, it's making up new ones.

We thought we signed a contract when we joined the WTO, but it's a contract whose terms keep changing. We put our country at the mercy of an entity whose rules and authority are constantly growing. Past administrations, both Democratic and Republican, have objected to WTO judges creating new rules and new obligations we never agreed to.

The Trump administration, fed up with U.S. complaints falling on deaf ears, stopped approving new judges in an effort to freeze the out-of-control Appellate Body process.

What did the WTO bureaucrats do in response? They went and created a whole new judicial body outside the agreed-upon rules without asking anyone—and used American taxpayer dollars to fund its operation.

The WTO's power grabs threaten America's sovereignty and national security.

Article XXI, the national security exception, reads: "Nothing in this Agreement shall be construed...to prevent any contracting party from taking any action which it considers necessary for the protection of its essential security interests."[31]

That's what the U.S. agreed to. What the agreement says is absolutely clear: we can take actions we consider to be in our national security interest and the WTO can't stop us.

If Washington determines it's vital to our national security interest to be able to produce steel and aluminum, we can take steps to stop China and other countries from dumping below-fair-market-value metals in the U.S. and driving American producers out of business.

But Eurocrats in Geneva believe it's up to their unelected "judges," not the elected government of United States, to decide what's in America's national security interest, no matter what we think Article XXI says.

Steven Vaughn served as counsel to the USTR. He says there's a fundamental problem with the WTO when we can read the exact same text and come to opposite conclusions.

"Somebody misunderstood what we all agreed to. We were told we had not given up any of our sovereignty," Vaughn says. "If we're this far apart just in terms of the basic concept, what is the point of trying to paper over them."[32]

How can you even talk about reforming an organization that doesn't understand the meaning of "cases will be settled within ninety days"? What good is rewriting rules with an outfit that doesn't follow rules?

Why bother to remain in the WTO?

It has done nothing to stop the greatest threat to world trade today: communist China's beggar-thy-neighbor predatory trade polices.

The Chinese Communist Party supports export industries with subsidies, tax breaks, export rebates, low-cost loans, and cheap inputs including a militarized workforce. The WTO has allowed Beijing to maintain its trade barriers even as we lowered ours. It continues to regard China, the world's second largest economy, as a "developing nation," as if it were no different than the Congo. And it requires the U.S. to treat a communist dictatorship whose economy depends on forced labor no differently than our democratic allies.

The WTO was part of a bold experiment to build a borderless, post-national world. President Clinton's Oxford roommate and Deputy Secretary of State Strobe Talbott saw the WTO, the International Monetary Fund, and the World Bank as "protoministries of trade, finance and development for a united world."

Well, the jury's back and the verdict is in: the experiment failed.

It's time to declare independence from the WTO, take control of our affairs, and rebuild the American middle class.

CHAPTER VIII

How to Hold China Accountable

Far too many drugs are currently made overseas, mostly in China and India. China is the world's main supplier of the active ingredients used in many common drugs from vitamin C to aspirin.

Moreover, foreign countries produce 90 percent of the active pharmaceutical ingredients (APIs) for essential medicines used in serious coronavirus infections, for example, according to Rosemary Gibson, co-author of *China Rx: Exposing the Risks of America's Dependence on China for Medicine.* Sedatives, antibiotics, anti-inflammatories, and medicines to control blood pressure are among the medications.

Bringing global supply chains back to the U.S. is the first step to ushering in a new era that would end our dangerous dependency on communist China for essential medicines and also break up the pharmaceutical oligarchy, whose single-minded pursuit of profits led to our dangerous drug dependency in the first place.

The trade association of the generic drug makers attacked Trump's trade and manufacturing czar Peter Navarro when he first advanced a plan for bringing pharmaceutical manufacturing back to the U.S. They clutched their precious global supply chains like pearls, falsely claiming that rearranging those chains would spike drug prices, forcing Americans to eat cat food or forgo their meds. In fact, these "global supply chains" are *not* the result of a free market economy: They are the *end product* of a global monopoly.

Chinese API companies formed a cartel that sold products below market price on the global market and drove many U.S., European, and Indian producers out of business. Once the Chinese gained dominant global market share, prices increased. American generic drug makers are happy to import active ingredients from abroad rather than make them.

We know it's possible to stand up to a trade competitor because we've deployed this strategy before. Take, for example, how the federal government turned the U.S. into the arsenal of democracy that won World War II.

Aluminum was essential to the war effort in that global conflict. But an international cartel led by Alcoa, itself a monopoly, controlled the supply of aluminum. When Alcoa refused to increase production to the level needed to build fifty thousand airplanes, the federal government lent millions to an upstart in the aluminum foil business named Richard Reynolds. That gave Reynolds the boost he needed to make more than tin foil, and it gave America the planes it needed to win the war.

In the current global conflict, Washington would be wise to ignore the wishes of the pharma oligarchs clinging to their global supply chains and bring drug manufacturing back home. That's what the American people want.

Americans Say U.S. Relies Too Heavily on Foreign Supply Chains

In May 2020, Bloomberg News released a poll showing, yet again, how hungry Americans are to bring manufacturing back to the United States, whatever the cost. An overwhelming 86 percent of respondents said the U.S. relies too heavily on foreign supply chains. In addition, the poll found:

- 40 percent said they won't buy products from China.
- 55 percent don't think China can be trusted to follow through on its trade-deal commitments signed in January 2020 to buy more U.S. products.
- 66 percent favor raising import restrictions over the pursuit of free trade deals as a better way to boost the U.S. economy.
- 78 percent would be willing to pay more for products if the company that made them moved manufacturing out of China.

These findings confirm other surveys. The Harris Poll[33] found 86 percent of Americans approve of companies that promise to move their manufacturing out of China and back to the United States. Pew Research Center[34] found more than seven in ten Americans don't trust Chinese Communist Party leader Xi Jinping, record disapproval for the Red dictator.

The globalists were shocked to find a supermajority of Americans supports protecting domestic industries. Chad Bown, a senior fellow at the free-trade-loving think tank Peterson Institute for International Economics, tried to explain it away by essentially accusing Americans of being racists, xenophobes, stupid, and otherwise bad, saying, "Foreigners are an all too easy political target in normal times. But once they become unpopular, politics can turn dangerous."

Chad, Americans know they were sold a bill of goods by smarty-pants "moderates" like you. It's really not that hard to understand: China took our jobs, and all we got in exchange was a virus that cancelled Easter and killed grandma. Saying "we need to collaborate with China" sounds a lot like "let's keep on kissing Xi's ass."

The overwhelming majority of Americans says no thanks, here's what we're gonna do instead: we'll make our own stuff, keep our jobs, and keep our money.

That's how we'll hold China accountable.

CHAPTER IX

Defund China!

Commentators and leaders of nations have said China should pay reparations for damage caused by the coronavirus pandemic.

There is no dispute the Chinese Communist Party deliberately withheld crucial information and hoarded protective supplies the world needed to prepare for the pandemic. Its actions caused both mortal and material damage.

Germany sent Beijing a bill for the costs. Good luck waiting for Beijing to pay.

But there are other ways to collect.

Consider: Every dollar the Chinese Communist Party would possibly pay us in damages would be a dollar we gave them beforehand.

We can save ourselves the trouble of trying to collect the bill *by not sending them the money in the first place.*

Let's say it out loud: Boycott China. Defund the CCP.

China's communist dictators have been waging economic warfare against us for decades, launching missiles from their mines, mills, and factories in an attack that has destroyed our industries as effectively as precision-guided munitions.

Now the pandemic has wrought further destruction. They have succeeded in literally stopping our way of life. We can't let them do that again.

How?

Just as the CCP has waged economic warfare against the U.S., we can do the same. The Chinese Communist Party lives off of the money we send them, and we send them a lot.

We must stop sending them our money. We must defund the CCP. Our *government* must defund the CCP.

We must cut off their access to U.S. taxpayer dollars. The U.S. government contributes to the World Bank, which gives the CCP billions. We funded the WHO, Beijing's puppet. We fund U.N. agencies controlled by the CCP. We fund scientific research in and with China. The National Institute of Health (NIH) even funded bat virus research in Wuhan[35] after it was banned in the U.S. (What could possibly go wrong with that? Oh wait, we found out.)

Wall Street must defund the CCP.

We must cut off its access to Western capital. Wall Street steers billions to CCP-controlled companies listed on American exchanges. It helps CCP-controlled entities sell securities in the U.S. Billions flow through index funds that include shares of Chinese companies. Pension funds from California to Iowa have staked the retirement savings of Americans on these dodgy investments.

The finance guys overseeing the federal Thrift Savings Plan—essentially a 401(k) plan for military personnel and federal workers—thought it would be a good idea to invest billions in a catalogue of Chinese companies that manufacture weapons, cyberespionage tools, and surveillance gear for the CCP. Right now, some of our largest state and union pension funds hand money over to these companies.

Corporate America must defund the CCP.

We must cut off its access to Western technology. American companies were warned to get out of China years ago. When we slapped tariffs on China's imports, American companies did Beijing's lobbying and squealed like stuck pigs. Everyone from Bible publishers to shoe salesmen pleaded penury and predicted doom if the tariffs weren't lifted immediately.

Had they diversified their supply chains as suggested, we wouldn't be in the situation we're in now, depending on a hostile regime for the goods we need to save our lives.

And *each one of us* has a part to play too.

When we say Boycott China, we are telling the CCP the American people are on to them. We know the dollars we send are being used to bury us—sometimes literally.

When we say Boycott China, we are telling American-in-name-only companies to get out of China—now. Whenever there is an alternative to Made in China, we will take it. We can buy New Balance athletic shoes instead of Nikes. We can buy from our local farmer or Hormel instead of Smithfield. We can hold off upgrading our iPhone until Tim Cook stops funding the CCP's techno-totalitarian dystopia. We're telling GM not to import Envision SUVs from China. We're telling Twitter to deplatform CCP propaganda mouthpieces, not Americans.

When we say Boycott China, we are telling Washington to stop sending our tax dollars to our mortal enemy—no excuses. We are telling elected officials like Senators Josh Hawley and Tom Cotton that we have their backs. And we're telling the others to stop peddling excuses, get a backbone, and stand up for America.

Don't let the CCP control our food (Smithfield); our media (CBS/Paramount, NBC/Universal, ABC/Disney, CNN/Warner, AMC theaters, Hollywood); our energy; and our technology.

When we say Boycott China, we are telling the CCP's apologists in big media, big banks, big corporations, and the Washington Swamp who sold out America and her people—time's up.

Our first war of independence began with boycotts of British goods following the Stamp Act, the Townshend Act, and the Tea Act.

The founders understood that America would not be truly independent if we relied on other nations for our manufactured goods.

With this boycott let us declare our independence from the tyrants of Beijing and the tyranny of globalism that brought us to the current impasse.

We can—we must—we will—stop giving China's dictators our money.

The way to hold the CCP accountable is to build our own stuff, not buy it from them.

To ensure we recover from the coronavirus pandemic, we must do two things:

Wash our hands, and wash our hands of China.

CHAPTER X

Common Sense on Communist China

The idea we propose—economic independence from China, national self-sufficiency, not globalism—is not presently fashionable enough to be accepted without explanation.

The fashionable status quo is accepted as right without being questioned or examined closely, and any argument in favor of altering it inevitably raises an outcry from the fashionable defenders of the "prevailing wisdom," however unwise it or they may be.

On these pages we offer simple facts, plain arguments, and common sense so that readers may determine for themselves the wisdom of the current course and the need to chart a new one, that is, the course of independence from the economic orbit of China.

Much has been written on the relationship between the United States and communist China, by many different authors with many different motives. But the debate is over.

The damage and degradations we have suffered as a result of our long-standing relationship with the People's Republic of

China and its ruling Communist Party demand a closer inspection of the status quo and a course correction.

The abuses we have suffered are irrefutable, insufferable, and intolerable. Our people had to be driven to wanting independence from China.

There was never a greater cause of greater importance. This is not the concern of a single city, state, class, race, or nation. This is not the preoccupation merely of a day, a year, or even an age. The outcome of the present conflict will determine the fate of humanity till the end of time.

Those opposing our declaration of independence argue that America has prospered from its relationship with China, and continuing this relationship is necessary for our future prosperity. That would be to say the past is prologue to the future, or the mother's milk that nourished us as infants should be our diet forever, or our teenage tastes will last throughout our lifetime. That is clearly absurd.

But some still oppose a divorce from Beijing. They say we must "collaborate" and "cooperate" with the communist regime going forward. Such "collaboration" and "cooperation" used to be called appeasement. And that's just what they are.

These collaborators, if you will, with the Communist Party of China fall roughly into four categories:

> *The Vested*: They cannot be trusted. They have a vested interest in continuing the status quo. Their power, prestige, and fortunes derive from commerce with China. In this category you will find the owners of our major media companies: Disney, the parent of ABC News, owns a theme park and distributes films in the People's Republic. Ditto NBC (Universal theme park/studio), CBS (Paramount studio) and CNN (Warner

Brothers theme park/studio). Like the NBA, they dare not offend Xi, who holds the purse strings. Fellow travelers include Wall Street bankers who earn billions from Chinese investments, consultants such as McKinsey & Company, and the import lobby, which includes everyone from Wal-Mart to the Apparel & Footwear Association. They have all grown fat from business with Red China. Commerce has weakened their spirit of patriotism.

The Weak: They *cannot* see the danger. They are comfortable in their ivory towers and are slaves to fear. They fear conflict, even conflict with prevailing thinking. The more they have to lose, the less willing they are to venture on a new path.

The Prejudiced: They *will not* see the danger. Their minds are made up—their hatred of Donald Trump blinded them to reality. When the former president called out the CCP, they reflexively took Beijing's side. They don't believe in the gender binary, but regarding Trump, their thinking is binary: if Trump is for it, they are against it and vice versa. In this camp count journalists such as those[36] who claim the former president's criticism of the CCP was an effort to deflect criticism of his own actions.

The "Moderates": These "reasonable" men and women think better of China's government than it deserves.

This last group is the most dangerous. They have done and will do more damage to our country and the cause of national economic independence than all of the other three.

These "moderates" enjoy a good life, well paid and comfortable in their protected professions.

From their sinecures in academia, media, think tanks, and government, they counsel collaboration with China's dictators and pray that we may be friends again. They dispense their moderate prescriptions on the pages of foreign policy journals and smooth their balms of moderation on policymakers and pundits.

They typically live in affluent coastal cities, far from the scenes of sorrow scarring our land, the devastated communities and vast tracts of our country laid waste by the economic warfare China is waging against America. They are strangers to the once prosperous cities and towns reduced to ruin and bereft of hope.

Being of a passive nature, they counsel a course of cooperation, collaboration with China, so that we may be friends again.

But is that possible?

Is it possible to love, honor, and engage in good faith with the power that has brought poverty and pestilence to your land?

If you can't, you're only kidding yourself to pretend otherwise. Your future relationship will not be honest. It will be based on expediency and convenience, not conviction, and will soon relapse into something far worse than the horribleness it was before.

Those who have not lost their jobs, their homes, their families, and their dignity should not judge those who have—and are now demanding a course correction.

And anyone who has had their home and livelihood taken away and still wants to shake hands with the thief is not a statesman but a coward.

The point here is not to shock or exaggerate but to wake us up. The Chinese Communist Party cannot conquer us unless we let ourselves be conquered by our own delay, hesitation, and timidity.

But the ruin and indignities we have suffered will be worth it if they awaken us to the dangers of continuing our dance with the devil. Without such an awakening, that dance will continue into the dark night. Reconciliation, cooperation, and collaboration is a dangerous delusion, a dream. It is collaboration in our own demise.

It is now clear that we must separate and chart a new course, our own course. The ties that bound us together have frayed beyond repair, and no amount of spin and artifice can restore them.

Reconciliation is not possible with wounds so deep.

We have tried every other means of repairing the relationship, and they've been fruitless. Negotiations, discussions, and "high-level working groups" have proven futile.

They have done nothing but confirm the CCP's conviction that we will let them get away with making empty promises, that they can continue with their abuses and tricks.

We must declare our independence. It is delusional to believe the Communist Party of China will fulfill the next deal, abide by the next agreement or the last one, or live up to whatever promise it makes or pact it strikes with us.

That's what we believed when we ran thousands of miles away to Geneva expecting the World Trade Organization to resolve our disputes.

Our petitions dragged on for months, then years, during which time our industries, the victims of communist China's predatory practices, were driven to bankruptcy and our people reduced to poverty.

We tried that route. It didn't work. Enough.

It is evident China and America have different systems. They are entitled to theirs, we to ours. But if we intertwine them, their system will strangle ours as would a python.

It is in the interest of America to be independent. Anything less will lead to greater problems in the future, problems far worse than what we have seen, and then the stakes will be so much higher. The consequences would not just be the temporary shutdown of our society, but the end of our self-governance, the permanent subjugation of our people to a foreign power whose dictatorial system is inimical to the freedoms we take as our birthright and the beliefs we hold in our hearts and in our immortal souls.

We are at a crossroads, and independence is the only way forward. We haven't come this far—paid the price those before us have paid; suffered the deprivations, indignities, and assaults simply to win a lawsuit before a Geneva tribunal whose judgment cannot be collected; tried in vain to extract another promise not worth the paper it's written on; or struck another deal whose terms, like those before, will never be honored—only to lose our country, our livelihoods, and our independence to a foreign power.

We must reject the hardened Pharaoh of Beijing with the pretended title "Father of the People" who slaughters his own family and sleeps with their blood on his soul.

What if we just kissed and made up, reconciled, as the moderates suggest in artful and hypocritical words appearing in newspapers of record and other outlets lacking judgment and honesty?

It would be the ruin of America. Beijing's rulers would retain control of manufacturing the goods our lives depend on. They would determine where they are made and at what price. We would be dependent on their whims for our medicine, our clothing, our steel, and, in the end, everything else.

Beijing would continue to have a veto over giving us what we need. As we saw during the pandemic, they would even decide if we live.

Should they decide we do live, they would control how we live—what we own, where we work, and what wages we are paid.

For decades, we have seen Beijing dictate: "You shall make no furniture, no shoes, no clothing, no toys, no automobile parts unless it is at the price we say, and if you try, we will undersell you and drive you out of business. Your people shall be paid no better than our prisoners or the laborer who lives with twelve others in her dormitory room in Shenzhen."

Nor do the dictates stop there. "And we will tell you what you can say. If you criticize the Communist Party of China, we will have your employer fire you and you will be blacklisted."

Under the relationship the moderates wish to retain, our own people make fewer and fewer of the goods we use, and more and more of the things we still produce are made on terms dictated in Beijing and favorable to Beijing.

After all is said in done, if we reconcile, cooperate, and collaborate with Beijing, we effectively will be as enslaved in our own country as if we were in a sweatshop or prison camp in China.

The goal of China's government is not to lift up our country, but to keep us as low as possible, subservient, dependent, and reliant on their power.

China's rulers seek to enhance the power and stature of China. Their policies are designed to promote their country's advantage and prosperity. They will suppress growth in our country every time our growth interferes with theirs.

America's interest will always come second, at best, to the interest of China's rulers.

Here's the key question: Is it wise to be at the mercy of such a power?

If you say no, you support independence. There is no other choice—it's either dependence or independence.

"We must seek collaboration and cooperation," say the moderate voices. "That is also what our friends across the Pacific want."

If China's rulers were to proclaim a policy of cooperation and collaboration, whether in public health, scientific research, or alleviating this or that global problem, it would be yet another deception like all those that have come before. Its purpose would be to convince us to reconcile and continue the relationship that has led to our national ruin.

Continuing our dependency on China on even the best of terms does not bode well for our future. It leads to government under the guardianship of Beijing, our economic destiny and even our freedoms determined by a faraway power.

No industry will want to establish itself here knowing its future, fortunes, and investment could be wiped out at any time by foreign privateers who flood our markets with destructively priced goods.

Millions of our citizens have already been ruined by China's economic warfare. Those who make our clothing, our cars, our steel have had their livelihoods taken from them. Their families and communities have been impoverished.

These Americans have nothing left but their liberty, their God-given freedoms, and their love of family, neighbor, community, and country. They have no desire to submit to the foreign power they have correctly identified as their tormentor.

If our government, in the name of cooperation, collaboration, and reconciliation, asked these Americans, who have lost so much to sacrifice what they hold in their hearts, it would invite their contempt and disdain and risk provoking open revolt in our nation.

Consider: If you lost your job, your home, your family to the profiteers of Beijing, the last thing you'd want to hear is "we must cooperate with our destroyers."

We must dedicate ourselves to independence now, or risk the rise of a future demagogue who will exploit the discontent and poverty of our people to overturn our system and trample our freedoms.

Those who oppose independence are opening the door to further turmoil and future tyranny, to stirring up division by race, by class, by ancestral national origin.

It's madness to talk of collaboration, cooperation, or partnership with a foreign government that has inflicted such damage and ruin upon our people and our nation.

Do we really expect the relationship will improve if we continue our cooperation? Do the collaborators truly believe this?

On what terms are we to collaborate with tormentors who ignore injustice and have shown they have not only the power to shut down our way of life but the willingness to use that power?

What would stop them from doing it again?

What concession, what "collaboration," would they expect from us—or, more to the point, would they extort from us—in order for them to forgo shutting down our society again?

Do we really believe things will get better if we continue down the path of collaboration and cooperation at the point of a bayonet? To those who say we must reconcile, collaborate, cooperate, can we forget the injuries and the indignities we've suffered? Can we forget the lies and infidelities?

Can we truly return to the naïve past? Can we restore lost innocence? Can we restore virginity? Can we forgive the rapist? Can we bring back what once was a proud, independent nation?

If we ignore injustice, if we let the robber and the murderer go unpunished, justice itself will disappear. We must defend what is right and stand up to what is wrong and unjust.

A cruel pursuer has hunted justice and freedom around the world. We must receive those who love freedom and demand justice, and grant these fugitives asylum for the good of all humanity.

There is no question that we must reset our relations and reestablish our independence. The question remaining is one of timing—when and how?

We can answer that question: The time is now.

The longer we wait, the harder it will be. The yoke we are under will be heavier, the CCP's military, technology, and factories will be stronger.

We have the people, the talents, and the resources to effect independence now.

Food, fiber, timber, energy, rich soil, and minerals lie within our borders. Our people have the talents and capital to combine them in sufficient quantities to fill our needs with surplus to sell to the rest of the world.

We have the largest consumer market, indeed the envy of the world. Our government buys more goods and services than entire nations.

No country on earth is blessed with a more favorable climate or resources, both human and natural, more abundant than our own. Why would we not use these?

To those who would say we must seek not independence and self-reliance but collaboration and cooperation with those who have so injured us, remember: conquest may be achieved under the pretense of friendship.

We have seen in our dealings with this foreign power that what we have not willingly and openly surrendered has been taken from us, and will be taken again. We will be cheated into slavery.

Developing our own industries is good economic policy and good defense policy. We have seen how abandoning our factories left us defenseless. When we use our riches to build our industries, we will never fear an external enemy.

Resolution is inherent to us. Courage is in our character. Our ancestors left family and familiar lands behind, risking all to leap into an unknown wilderness. Why do we hesitate to take the next, necessary step?

If we allow our destiny to be determined by Beijing rather than by our own hearts, if we allow our nation to be ruled from afar, it will be a nation not worth living in.

The current weakness and the underdevelopment of our own industries is, in fact, an argument for our independence. It means there is so much yet to be developed, so many opportunities for growth and innovation. As capital rushed to China to build industries there, it will do so here.

There are many reasons why we must declare our independence. Here are just some.

First, no one will do it for us. We cannot rely on the World Trade Organization, the United Nations, NATO, the World Bank, the World Court or some other authority, or our allies to solve our problems with the CCP. Some of these institutions have no interest in a strong self-sufficient America. They are components of the existing order that China's government has successfully manipulated and hijacked.

Second, our independence will set an example for others seeking alternatives to the CCP-led globalist order.

By declaring our intention for independence openly, we can begin to build national self-sufficiency as an alternative to the globalist order that has injured not just us but all nations and peoples. We can enter into honest, fair, and reciprocal trade with other nations and negotiate open agreements openly arrived at.

As strange and difficult as this challenge seems to some, it must be done, and the sooner the better. Once we begin, it will soon become familiar and agreeable, and doable. If we don't, we will be haunted by the nagging feeling of putting off some important business that we know must be done and wish would go away. Worse, we will be destined to live in continuing servitude to the CCP.

It is now the interest of America to provide for herself.

No nation in a state of foreign dependence can achieve material eminence, opulence, or prosperity.

If we wish to preserve our country, our freedom, and our values uncontaminated by the corruption of the CCP, we must have a separation, we must have independence.

Now is the time to reassert our independence. The longer we delay, the deeper our dependence will become, to the point where we will be as bereft of industries and know-how as a Third World resource colony.

Independence is straightforward. We can achieve it ourselves, on our terms, by our own design. We can determine our destiny.

Collaboration, dependence along the existing lines, is complicated, complex, and requires the consent of another. As we have discovered, the partner we are engaged with has proven to be deceptive, unreliable, and untrustworthy. Why should we place our fate in such hands?

The present state of America is alarming, with too few jobs for our people, our industries weakened, our nation dependent on foreign sources for essential goods.

The situation is without precedent.

If something isn't done now, it will be too late to do anything.

The Chinese Communist Party seeks to divide us from our allies and from each other, and it's doing quite a good job.

Read the *New York Times* and *Washington Post*, watch the cable news channels and you'll find commentators dispensing neither reasoned judgment nor honesty.

These pundits are well paid, secure, and soft. They should put themselves in the position of the machinists, the toolmakers, the factory workers, and the ranchers who lost their income and property and who saw their livelihood and future swept away by a flood of destructively priced imports.

To those who say let us return to where we were before the pandemic opened our eyes, I say, How can we trust a corrupt and faithless government that has lied to us and the entire world, and how can we trust such a criminal conspiracy to hold up its end of any bargain we strike with it in the future?

We must act now in this favorable time when we can see clearly what is before us and ignore those who are habitually opposed to national independence.

Some honestly fear independence because no plan has been laid out. They do not see a way out of our present condition, though they admit and accept that a new arrangement would be better.

On the following pages, we offer proposals and positive steps to the way forward. Others will offer yet more ideas. The most capable among us can collect these suggestions and form a useful and effective plan of action.

Declaring Independence: Proposals for a Plan of Action

First, we need to identify the industries where we face shortfalls. Experts in health care, defense, telecommunications, and other industries can catalogue the goods we currently produce

ourselves, what we can source from allies, and what is only available from China.

Second, we need to give incentives for businesses to move
away from China and come here. Just as China gave incentives to
move there, we can provide incentives to come back.

Making the current tariffs permanent would signal there is no
going back to the status quo ante. Additional tariffs would make
China a less attractive place to do business.

We can provide a tax write-off and streamlined regulatory
approvals for new plants built in the United States. Japan is offer-
ing companies cash to relocate from China.

We can leverage the purchasing power of the federal government. "Buy American" was once the rule for the federal government. Government contracts, a guaranteed buyer, provided
startup funding that nurtured aviation, telecommunications, and
other industries.

Most importantly, we must unify.

We must bring Democrats and Republicans, Progressives,
Conservatives, and Independents together and stand as one country against the Chinese Communist Party and its agents trying to
sow division among us.

Let us put our differences and suspicions aside and unite as
citizens and neighbors in this land.

Our plan and our wish is for peace with the people of China.
We seek to dissolve a bond that has caused misery to our people
and hers, that has impoverished our people and empowered a
tyrant over hers.

Those who say we can't be independent of communist China
are wrong.

Just as we declared independence from the British Empire, the greatest power on earth 247 years ago, we can restore our independence today.

We have it in our power to begin the world over again.

CHAPTER XI

Restoring Our Economic Independence

Communist China does not have our best interest at heart, to put it mildly. Americans understand it has become necessary to loosen the bonds that have tied us to the Communist regime in China.

Americans understand it has become necessary to do as we did more than two centuries ago: cut our ties to a foreign tyranny and establish our independence. Some honestly fear the independence because no plan has been laid out. They do not see a way out of our present condition, though they admit and accept that a new arrangement would be better.

On the following pages, we offer proposals and positive steps to the way forward. Others will offer yet more ideas. The most capable among us can collect these suggestions and form a useful and effective plan of action.

What We Propose

Here are three categories of things we must do: Identify, Incentify, and Unify.

Identify

First, we need to identify those industries that are critical to sustaining our way of life and identify where there are potential shortfalls in supply. For what products are we entirely or overly dependent on China?

Experts in the health care, electronics, telecommunications, automotive, defense, and other industries will catalogue what (and how much of it) we make in America, what we can buy from allies, and what we now buy from China and will need to replace. For example, we know that five of our ten top imports from China are available from Mexico.

Incentify

Second, we need to give entrepreneurs and businesses incentives to move their factories out of China and back to the United States. China gave businesses incentives to move there. We can give them incentives to move back.

We now have temporary tariffs on goods coming from China. Making the current tariffs permanent would signal there is no going back to the status quo ante, to the old way of doing business with the Communist Party of China. We should consider additional tariffs to offset the costs to American companies of environmental, health, labor, and safety laws; that would make China a less attractive place to do business.

Once corporate CEOs realize there's no going back to China, they can get down to the job of building new plants somewhere else.

We prefer they be built in the United States. But some might be built in Mexico or Central America. Even that would be better for our people, and not only because it would starve the CCP of the money its uses to subvert America.

Garment workers making T-shirts in El Salvador would be using cloth woven in North Carolina from cotton grown in Mississippi. And our neighbors to the south won't be so eager to rush our border if they can earn a living in their ancestral homes.

We can give patriotic companies an immediate 100 percent tax write-off for capital expenditures on new plants and equipment in the United States. Call it the Patriot Bonus.

We can streamline the regulatory process to fast-track approval for patriot companies building new plants in the U.S. to put Americans to work. These plants would utilize the latest advanced manufacturing technology.

We saw how outdated regulations and clunky bureaucracy held us back during the pandemic emergency. The Centers for Disease Control and Prevention (CDC) stopped states from testing. Doctors couldn't get face masks because rules said the elastic bands that held them in place were past their due date. Now, we have another emergency, and we can't let a "by the book" attitude hold us back. We have to rewrite the book.

We can leverage federal purchasing power to promote the reshoring of pharmaceutical and medical equipment supply chains. Our own taxpayer dollars can be the rocket fuel that launches the next generation of American industry.

That's how we used to do it. U.S. law required the Pentagon to Buy American when it went shopping. Federal contracts supported everything from basic industries such as steel, aluminum, and shipbuilding to entire new industries, including telecom, aerospace, and even personal computers. Steve Jobs and Steve Wozniak built the first Apple computers from surplus circuit boards and microchips originally made for the military, in America, with taxpayer dollars.

Today, the U.S. Departments of Defense, Veterans Affairs, and Health and Human Services buy huge amounts of pharmaceuticals and medical devices. Those and other federal agencies can provide a guaranteed market for a company to manufacture these goods in the U.S.A.

That would work for other industries too. The government is a huge buyer of cars, trucks, LED lights, furniture, building materials, office supplies, electronics, and a host of other goods and services. We can put our tax dollars to work putting our fellow citizens to work.

Here's another incentive: use government financing to help patriot companies build the U.S.A. If Wall Street would rather invest in China than in the U.S., the federal government can use our tax dollars to provide financing to companies to invest in America.

We've done it before and we can do it again.

Another incentive: Let's have the same set of honest and consistent accounting rules for Chinese and American companies. American businesses have to open their books to regulators to investors against fraud. But Chinese companies aren't required to open their books even though they're raising money from American investors. That doesn't make sense. Why should honest American businesses have to compete for investors' dollars against Chinese businesses that hide their books?

In addition, global companies headquartered in the U.S. need to be transparent about their investments in China. The fact is, these companies cannot get their cash out of China. Those assets are illiquid and should be counted as such (Level 3 assets in accounting parlance). Honest accounting would affect the company's valuation and stock price—and that would directly affect executive compensation. Honest accounting would be a strong incentive for executives to invest in America rather than the People's Republic of China.

While we're talking about equal enforcement of our laws, let's consider how Chinese companies openly flout the strict health, safety, environmental, child labor, minimum wage, and workplace laws American companies have to meet. That's unfair to Americans who play by the rules.

Importing goods produced without regard to these standards is a slap in the face to the generations before us who fought to gain decent working conditions and improve our standard of living.

In fact, the Tariff Act of 1930 makes it illegal to import goods produced "even in part" by forced labor or child labor. Enforcing our laws would be a strong disincentive to move jobs to China—and an incentive to keep them here.

Unify

Most importantly, we must unify.

We must bring together those of every political stripe—Democrats, Republicans, Progressives, Conservatives, and Independents—so that we stand together as one unified country. Make no mistake, the Chinese Communist Party and its agents are trying to sow division among us.

Unify means helping those who are going to be hurt so no one bears too heavy a burden in what will be a long fight. We've seen that with farmers who knew they had to sacrifice in the short term for the sake of building a better future. Black Americans and women were hurt disproportionately when good-paying jobs were sent to China; they will gain when those jobs come home.

Bringing manufacturing back to America is the key to ending income inequality and solving our chronic deficits.

Call to Action

Each one of us must urge our representatives and senators in Congress to support greater national self-sufficiency, beginning with crucial medical supplies but not ending there.

Congress can require the federal government to Buy American and Hire American when it spends taxpayer money.

Congress should hold companies controlled by the CCP to the same accounting and transparency standards as American companies.

It should require individuals and companies profiting from Chinese government-approved investments in China to register as foreign agents of Beijing.

Pension funds, private or public, should not invest retirees' savings in Chinese companies since they do not abide by our securities laws.

The government should enforce the laws that forbid the importation or sale of goods made wholly or in part with forced labor or child labor.

Congress and our elected representatives at the state and local level must remember they have a duty to serve We the People of the United States.

Those who say we can't be independent from China are wrong.

We declared our independence from the British Empire 247 years ago. We can restore our independence today.

National self-sufficiency will bring our communities prosperity instead of poverty. It will bring Americans work and dignity instead of drugs and despair.

Self-reliance is the ability to provide for oneself and one's family.

That is the solid foundation for liberty as individuals, self-governance as a people, and security as a nation.

We can do this. We must do this. And we will be better and stronger for it.

CHAPTER XII

A New Declaration of Independence

We hold these truths to be self-evident, that all men are created equal, that they are endowed by their Creator with certain unalienable Rights, that among these are Life, Liberty, and the pursuit of Happiness.

To secure these rights, We the People of the United States have instituted a Government that derives its just powers from the consent of the governed.

When in the Course of human events, it becomes necessary for one people to dissolve the bands which have connected them with another, and to resume the separate and equal status to which the Laws of Nature and Nature's God entitle them, we owe it to our fellows at home and around the world to explain the reasons why we separating.

We do not take this step hastily. We are not changing the existing order for trivial reasons. We have tolerated repeated indignities and injuries.

This long train of abuses has drained our people's wealth, sapped their health, and crushed their spirit. These abuses were all designed to achieve the same end: to reduce our independence and place us at the mercy of a foreign despotism.

With that knowledge, it is our right, indeed our duty, to alter the relations that led to our suffering and chart a new course to ensure our happiness and security.

Such has been the suffering that compels us to revise a contract that has served us so poorly.

The history of the Chinese Communist Party is a story of repeated injuries and violations. Its relations with the United States have had the effect of reducing us to dependency on its absolute tyranny.

To prove this, let the Facts be submitted for the world to review.

The CCP has refused to honor the obligations and terms of the contracts it has entered into with us.

It has neglected to correct its failures after they were pointed out and after promising to do so.

It has stolen the inventions, property, and designs of our people and profited from such theft.

It has flooded our land with substandard goods and foodstuffs which have endangered the health of our people.

It has spied on our people, hacked our computers, and robbed our personal information.

It has coerced our inventors into surrendering their discoveries without compensation, and then profited from the purloined property.

It has exported deadly drugs to our shores and killed thousands of our people, then refused to arrest the murderers responsible for making these poisons.

It has targeted our domestic industries for extinction and employed nefarious and illegal practices, including theft, espionage, and counterfeiting, to damage our people and their commerce.

It has used government-owned and -subsidized companies, in violation of all laws and internationally recognized standards, to gain an unfair and illegal advantage in commerce in order to drive American companies into bankruptcy.

It has distorted and perverted international commerce by debasing its currency to disadvantage American goods in the U.S. and around the world.

It has subverted honest commerce and robbed our people of subsistence through bribery, subsidies, theft, extortion, and counterfeiting of American goods.

It has bribed American scientists, doctors, and academics to turn over the findings of their research whose proper owner is the American people.

It has dispatched hordes of spies disguised as businessmen to our shores to steal the inventions of the companies that employ them.

It has dispatched spies disguised as journalists and diplomats to spread lies and sow division among our people.

It has threatened the employees and property of Americans doing business in the People's Republic of China.

It has sought to undermine the freedom of our academic institutions and pressured them to deny students the freedoms of speech and assembly we are endowed with by our Creator as unalienable rights.

It has through incompetence, corruption, and malice caused a deadly virus to be unleashed on our people, inflicting death and incalculable damage on our families, communities, and way of life.

It has deliberately spread lies about the nature of the disease, misleading the world and our people.

It failed to notify authorities of the deadly pathogen that they knew would spread around the world.

It arrested the brave doctors who first detected the disease, and forced them to deny the deadly infection was spreading.

It has destroyed records and samples of the virus the world needed to prepare a defense against the disease.

It has refused to allow the world's best scientific minds access to the city where the outbreak began, preventing a timely response and containment of the biological disaster.

It bought up the epidemic control equipment the world would need and hoarded it in China, leaving the world defenseless.

It has withheld those crucial supplies necessary to battle the disease which they caused to be loosed upon the world, causing additional deaths and suffering.

It has made authorities at the World Health Organization and other international administrative bodies dependent on China for their offices, salary, and tenure.

It has abused these administrative bodies at places unusual and distant, for the sole purpose of prolonging deliberations and fatiguing us into compliance with their measures.

It has ignored the rulings of duly appointed authorities that opposed the CCP's abuses and violations.

It has blocked the appointment of honest officials who would be justly inclined to oppose the CCP's ongoing violations and abuses.

It has enacted a multitude of new edicts preventing our people from doing commerce in China, and sent swarms of Officers to harass our people there and rob their substance.

It has kept among us Armies of spies and agents of influence without the knowledge and consent of our legislatures and authorities.

It has rendered their Military superior to the Civil power and required all businesses in China to obey the edicts of the tyrant.

It has combined with others to subject us to international authorities with laws foreign to our Constitution, and contrary to our own laws; requiring we assent to their rulings:

For requiring us to trade on unfavorable and unfair terms with China and all parts of the world;

For imposing expenditures on our Treasury without our Consent;

For quartering large bodies of spies among us;

For subjecting our commercial enterprises to be subject to unaccountable judges and tribunals;

For going overseas to faraway places to adjudicate alleged offences;

For abolishing our System of Laws and replacing it with an Arbitrary authority that expands it powers without our consent, making it an instrument for extending the CCP's absolute rule;

For taking away our Constitution, abolishing our Laws, and altering fundamentally our Forms of Governments; and

For overruling our own Legislatures, and declaring themselves invested with power to legislate for us.

It has abdicated the right to our partnership by declaring hostility to our values and waging Economic, Psychological, and Ideological War against us.

It has plundered our industries, ravaged our farms and fisheries, gutted our towns and cities, and destroyed the lives of our people.

It is at this time dispatching large Armies of agents to infiltrate, subvert, and take over our universities, industries, and research laboratories, seeking the desolation and subjugation of our people, with a cruelty & perfidy scarcely paralleled in the most barbarous ages, and totally unworthy of the government of a civilized nation.

It has constrained our fellow citizens with commercial interests in their country, coercing the leaders of our business, culture and sports industries to turn on our nation and do the bidding of the CCP.

It has fomented divisions among our people, spreading disinformation to create conflicts between races, sexes, and ethnic groups to effect the destruction of our society through unrestricted warfare.

In every stage of these Oppressions we have patiently petitioned for redress in the most reasonable terms. Our repeated Petitions have been answered only by empty promises and continued injury. A Government that behaves in such a manner is indeed unfit to be a partner with a free people.

We have no argument or dispute with the Chinese people. We have warned them the Chinese Communist Party seeks to extend its unwarranted power over us.

We appeal to their sense of justice and magnanimity, and we have asked them to correct these violations which would inevitably interrupt our commercial connections. We ask them to listen to the voice of justice and common interest. The people of China have been victims of the same Tyrant that seeks to tyrannize us.

We, therefore, appealing to the Supreme Judge of the world for the rectitude of our intentions, in the Name, and by Authority of the good People of these United States, solemnly publish and declare, That these United States of America, as a Free, Independent, and Sovereign Nation, are Absolved from dictates by any authority not elected by the People of the United States, and that the imbalanced economic dependence between our nation and the People's Republic of China shall be dissolved; and that as a Free and Independent Nation, we have full Power and Right to contract Alliances and establish Commerce to our advantage as we determine it to be, as all Independent states have a right to do.

And for the support of this Declaration, with a firm reliance on the protection of divine Providence, we mutually pledge to each other our Lives, our Fortunes, and our sacred Honor.

AFTERWORD

Americans lived in a global economy when we wrote the first Declaration of Independence.

We bought our clothing, our steel, and all our essential needs from Britain, then the workshop of the world. We knew the cost of dependence on a foreign power and didn't like it.

George Washington, Thomas Jefferson, Alexander Hamilton, and Thomas Paine decided America should be an independent country. Better to govern ourselves and make our own rules.

The American Revolution was a rebellion against globalism.

Today's "workshop of the world" is not Britain, but the People's Republic of China. And just as the King of England sought to cripple American industry, the rulers of China seek to drive American industry into extinction.

The pandemic showed us that we've grown dangerously dependent on others for our health, our well-being, and our way of life. Americans could not get the medical supplies we needed.

And it's not just medicines. Clothing, computers, and appliances are all made abroad. We are at the mercy of the country where our factories have moved.

For most of our nation's history, we were self-reliant. Our dependence didn't happen overnight. It took decades and was the result of decisions, deception, complacency, and delusion.

It doesn't have to be this way. It's time to do once again as we did two centuries ago. It's time to cut our ties to a foreign tyrant and reassert America's independence.

ACKNOWLEDGMENTS

I want to thank Jack Davis, a great American and the founder and chairman emeritus of I Squared R Element Inc., for his dedication to saving American jobs, farms, and industries. His patriotism, decency, and commitment to his employees, community, and country, and his belief in the American system of economic nationalism and national self-sufficiency, have changed our nation. His inspiration, work, and dedication to our country and the American people made this book possible.

This book is in many ways a CliffsNotes version of *The Great Betrayal*, Patrick J. Buchanan's account of economic nationalism, free trade, and their battle over the course of the history of our republic. It is the source for many of the quotes that appear in this book and has served as a reference book for my writing over the years. I highly recommend the full version.

NOTES

1   "Generalized System of Preferences (GSP)," Office of the United States Trade Representative, accessed June 26, 2020, https://ustr.gov/issue-areas/trade-development/preference-programs/generalized-system-preference-gsp

2   "About GSP," United Nations Conference on Trade and Development, accessed June 28, 2020, https://unctad.org/system/files/official-document/itcdtsbmisc58rev3_en.pdf

3   David Barboza, "How China Built iPhone City," New York Times online, Dec. 29, 2016, https://www.nytimes.com/2016/12/29/technology/apple-iphone-china-foxconn.html

4   George H. W. Bush, letter to Deng Xiaoping, quoted in "Document of 1989: President Bush's Secret Letter to Deng Xiaoping," Standoff At Tiananmen online, published June 12, 2012, http://www.standoffattiananmen.com/2012/06/document-of-1989-president-bushs-secret.html

5   William R. Hawkins, "Donald Trump, George HW Bush, and China," American Thinker online, Dec. 5, 2019, https://www.americanthinker.com/articles/2019/12/donald_trump_george_hw_bush_and_china.html

6   Michael Pillsbury, The Hundred-Year Marathon: China's Secret Strategy to Replace America as the Global Superpower, New York: Henry Holt and Company, 2015.

7   Maxim Kniazkov, "China Channeled Donations to US Politicians in 1996," Agence France Presse online, Aug. 11, 2001, https://sgp.fas.org/news/2001/08/afp081101.html

8   "To Authorize Extension of Nondiscriminatory Treatment to the People's Republic of China–Continued," S8369, 106th Cong., 2nd sess., Congressional Record, vol. 146, no. 106, Sept. 12, 2000: S8369-S8370.

9   Stephen Frank, "Sen. Dianne Feinstein's Ties to China Go Way Deeper than an Alleged Office Spy," California Political Review online, Aug. 9, 2018, http://www.capoliticalreview.com/capoliticalnewsandviews/sen-dianne-feinsteins-ties-to-china-go-way-deeper-than-an-alleged-office-spy/

10   Richard N. Gardner, "The Hard Road to World Order," Foreign Affairs, vol. 52, no. 3, April 1974, https://www.foreignaffairs.com/world/hard-road-world-order

11   "Treaty Establishing the European Community as Amended by Subsequent Treaties," Hellenic Resources Network, March 25, 1957, accessed June 28, 2020, http://www.hri.org/docs/Rome57/

12   Michael Pillsbury, The Hundred-Year Marathon.

13   Maxim Kniazkov, "China Channeled Donations to US Politicians."

14   Benson Lossing, "What Caused the Boston Tea Party?" Our Country: Household History for All Readers, New York: Johnson, Wilson & Co., 1887, accessed June 28, 2020, http://www.publicbookshelf.com/public_html/Our_Country_vol_2/whatcause_db.html

15 Thomas Jefferson, "From Thomas Jefferson to David Humphreys, 20 January 1809," Founders Online, National Archives, accessed June 28, 2020, https://founders.archives.gov/documents/Jefferson/99-01-02-9596

16 Thomas Jefferson, "Thomas Jefferson to Jean Baptiste Say, 2 March 1815," Founders Online, National Archives, accessed June 28, 2020, https://founders.archives.gov/documents/Jefferson/03-08-02-0242

17 Thomas Jefferson, "Thomas Jefferson to Benjamin Austin, 9 January 1816," Founders Online, National Archives, accessed June 28, 2020, https://founders.archives.gov/documents/Jefferson/03-09-02-0213

18 Henry Carey, The Harmony of Interests: Agricultural, Manufacturing, & Commercial, 1868, London: Forgotten Books, 2018, p. 59, https://www.forgottenbooks.com/en/books/The_Harmony_of_Interests_Agricultural_Manufacturing_and_Commercial_1000261623

19 Henry Carey, "VI–How Protection Affects Commerce," in excerpts from The Harmony of Interests: 1851, pp. 71–72, accessed June 28, 2020, http://www.let.rug.nl/usa/documents/1851-1875/the-harmony-of-interests/index.php

20 Speeches and Addresses of William McKinley from His Election to Congress to the Present Time, 1894, Library of Congress, p. 376, accessed June 28, 2020, https://babel.hathitrust.org/cgi/pt?id=loc.ark:/13960/t6833w058&view=1up&seq=386

21 Henry Carey, "Conclusion," in excerpts from The Harmony of Interests: 1851, pp. 228–229, accessed June 28, 2020, http://www.let.rug.nl/usa/documents/1851-1875/the-harmony-of-interests/conclusion.php

22 Adam Smith, "Of Restraints upon the Importation from Foreign Countries of Such Goods as Can Be Produced at

Home," in An Inquiry into the Nature and Causes of the Wealth of Nations, Book IV, Ch. II, accessed June 28, 2020, https://www.econlib.org/library/Smith/smWN. html?chapter_num=27#book-reader

23 Jess Bravin and Louise Radnofsky, "Court Backs Obama on Health Law," Wall Street Journal online, June 29, 2012, https://www.wsj.com/articles/SB10001424052702304898704 577480371370927862

24 David Ricardo, On the Principles of Political Economy and Taxation, London: John Murray, 1817, accessed June 28, 2020, https://books.google.com/books?id=cUBKAAAAYAAJ &dq=editions%3Ay8vXR4oK9R8C&pg=PR1#v=onepage &q&f=true

25 Josh Hawley, "The W.T.O. Should Be Abolished," New York Times online, May 5, 2020, https://www.nytimes. com/2020/05/05/opinion/hawley-abolish-wto-china.html

26 Richard N. Gardner, "The Hard Road to World Order," p. 558.

27 "The Process–Stages in a Typical WTO Dispute Settlement Case: 6.5 Appellate Review," World Trade Organization, accessed June 28, 2020, https://www.wto.org/english/tratop_e/ dispu_e/disp_settlement_cbt_e/c6s5p4_e.htm

28 James Bacchus and Simon Lester, "Trade Justice Delayed Is Trade Justice Denied: How to Make WTO Dispute Settlement Faster and More Effective," CATO Institute, Nov. 20, 2019, https://www.cato.org/publications/free-trade-bulletin/trad e-justice-delayed-trade-justice-denied

29 "United States–Countervailing Measures on Supercalendered Paper from Canada, Communication from the United States," World Trade Organization, April 17, 2020, https:// docs.wto.org/dol2fe/Pages/SS/directdoc.aspx?filename=q:/ WT/DS/505-12.pdf&Open=True

30 "USTR Robert Lighthizer Statement on the WTO Panel
Report in Canada's Challenge to U.S. Countervailing Duties
on Supercalendered Paper," Office of the United States
Trade Representative, July 6, 2018, https://ustr.gov/about-us/
policy-offices/press-office/press-releases/2018/july/ustr-rober
t-lighthizer-statement-wto

31 William Alan Reinsch and Jack Caporal, "The WTO's First
Ruling on National Security: What Does It Mean for the
United States?" Center for Strategic and International Studies,
April 5, 2019, https://www.csis.org/analysis/wtos-first-rulin
g-national-security-what-does-it-mean-united-states

32 Soumaya Keynes, Chad P. Bown, and Stephen Vaughn, "111:
Trade Policy Under Trump," Nov. 25, 2019, Trade Talks
podcast, produced by Peterson Institute for International
Economics, 52:07, https://www.tradetalkspodcast.com/podca
st/111-trade-policy-under-trump/

33 Josh Rogin, "The Coronavirus Crisis Is Turning Americans
in Both Parties Against China," Washington Post online,
accessed June 28, 2020, https://www.washingtonpost.com/
opinions/2020/04/08/coronavirus-crisis-is-turning-american
s-both-parties-against-china/

34 Kat Devlin, Laura Silver, and Christine Huang, "U.S. Views of
China Increasingly Negative Amid Coronavirus Outbreak,"
Pew Research Center, April 21, 2020, https://www.pewre-
search.org/global/2020/04/21/u-s-views-of-china-increasing-
ly-negative-amid-coronavirus-outbreak/

35 Christina Lin, "Why US Outsourced Bat Virus Research
to Wuhan," Asia Times online, accessed April 22, 2020,
https://asiatimes.com/2020/04/why-us-outsourced-bat-viru
s-research-to-wuhan/

36 Deb Riechmann and Zeke Miller, "Trump's Anti-China Rhetoric Aimed at Boosting US Leverage," Associated Press online, accessed May 4, 2020, https://apnews.com/e981e084208ec5dc3c93d9e5b5ae234a

FURTHER READING

Patrick J. Buchanan, *The Great Betrayal: How American Sovereignty and Social Justice are Being Sacrificed to the Gods of the Global Economy*, Boston: Little Brown & Company, 1995.

Michael Pillsbury, *The Hundred-Year Marathon: China's Secret Strategy to Replace America as the World's Superpower*, New York: Henry Holt and Company, 2015.

Peter Navarro and Greg Autry, *Death by China: Confronting the Dragon—A Global Call to Action*, Hoboken, N.J.: Prentice Hall, 2011.

Rosemary Gibson, *China Rx*, Amherst, N.Y.: Prometheus Books, 2018.

Clyde Prestowitz, *The Betrayal of American Prosperity*, New York: Free Press, 2010.

Rob Spalding, *Stealth War: How China Took Over While America's Elite Slept*, New York: Portfolio, 2019.

Bill Gertz, *Deceiving the Sky: Inside Communist China's Drive for Global Supremacy*, New York: Encounter Books, 2019.

Eamonn Fingleton, *In Praise of Hard Industries: Why Manufacturing, Not the Information Economy, is the Key to Future Prosperity*, Boston: Houghton Mifflin, 1999.

Ian Fletcher, *Free Trade Doesn't Work: What Should Replace It and Why*, U.S. Business & Industry Council, 2010.

Ha-Joon Chang, *Bad Samaritans: The Myth of Free Trade and the Secret History of Capitalism*, London: Bloomsbury Press, 2008.

Brett Kingstone, *The Real War Against America*, New York: Specialty Publishing/Max King LLC, 2005.

Qiao Liang and Wang Xiangsui, *Unrestricted Warfare*, Beijing: PLA Literature and Arts Publishing House, 1999.

Matt Stoller, *Goliath: The 100-Year War Between Monopoly Power and Democracy*, New York: Simon & Schuster, 2019.

William Hawkins, articles and blog posts at *American Thinker*, www.americanthinker.com

Some Twitter accounts to follow:

Dan DiMicco @DanRDimicco
Christopher Balding @BaldingsWorld
Kyle Bass @Jkylebass
Robert Spalding @robert_spalding
Alan Tonelson @alantonelson
Matthew Stoller @matthewstoller

ABOUT THE AUTHOR

Curtis Ellis served as senior policy adviser on Donald Trump's 2016 presidential campaign; he was on the presidential transition team, and in the U.S. Department of Labor, and served as senior policy director for America First Policies. He founded the non-profit American Jobs Alliance in 2011 promoting "Buy American and Hire American" policies. He was one of the strongest voices opposing America's membership in the jobs-endangering Trans-Pacific Partnership trade agreement in 2015. Ellis was a true patriot and fervent crusader for the American worker. His activism and cogent thinking initiated the policies that brought manufacturing plants and jobs back to America. Mr. Ellis was an astute architect of economic nationalism. He was at the forefront of the "great awakening" to China's trade abuse and economic warfare aimed at weakening our nation, and he dutifully spread the message through journalism, television, and other forums throughout his career.

Ellis worked in media, politics, and government at the local, state, national, and international levels. In the course of his career, he worked on political campaigns; served as media liaison for the New York State Senate Central Staff; served as communications director for a Democratic member of the House of Representatives on Capitol Hill; and toiled in the trenches of broadcast, print, and online media as a writer, producer, reporter, and political commentator.

Mr. Ellis regularly appeared on Fox, Newsmax, and other networks; previously wrote for CNN and MSNBC; and wrote for publications including the *Financial Times*, *Time* magazine, *Huffington Post*, Breitbart, the Daily Caller, the *American Conservative*, and *American Greatness*. He produced stories for *60 Minutes*, NPR, NBC, and HBO and was heard regularly on radio stations across the country. He was a member of the Writers Guild of America, East, an AFL-CIO affiliate.